Supermarket for Rural Customers

Published by
ACADEMIC FOUNDATION
in association with

Sardar Patel Institute of Economic and Social Research
Ahmedabad

ABOUT THE AUTHOR:

Subrata Dutta is an Associate Professor at the Sardar Patel Institute of Economic and Social Research (an ICSSR Institute) in Ahmedabad, India. His research focuses on entrepreneurship, rural industrialisation, and economics of rural growth linkages, among others. He received his PhD degree in Social Sciences (Economics) from Wageningen University in the Netherlands, and has published papers in national and international journals.

Munish Alagh is currently a Senior Fellow of Indian Council of Social Science Research, based at Sardar Patel Institute of Economic and Social Research, Ahmedabad. He has completed his Phd from University of Mumbai in the area of agricultural markets and price response. He has written three books and a number of articles in reputed journals, which have been received very well. His academic papers have been published in reputed Indian journals such as Economic and Political Weekly, Indian Journal of Agricultural Economics etc. He has been teaching and doing research in reputed institutes for the last 20 years, including 10 years as a faculty of Economics in Ahmedabad University's MBA department.

Supermarket for Rural Customers

A Study of a Community-Oriented Social Enterprise in Gujarat

Subrata Dutta and Munish Alagh

ACADEMIC FOUNDATION
NEW DELHI

www.academicfoundation.org

First published in 2017
by

ACADEMIC FOUNDATION
4772-73 / 23 Bharat Ram Road, (23 Ansari Road),
Darya Ganj, New Delhi - 110 002 (India).
Phones : 23245001 / 02 / 03 / 04.
Fax : +91-11-23245005.
E-mail : books@academicfoundation.com
www.academicfoundation.org

in association with
Sardar Patel Institute of Economic and Social Research, Ahmedabad.

Disclaimer:
The findings/views/opinions expressed in this book are solely those of the authors and do not necessarily reflect the views of the publisher.

Cataloging in Publication Data--DK
Courtesy: D.K. Agencies (P) Ltd. <docinfo@dkagencies.com>

Dutta, Subrata, author.
Supermarket for rural customers: a study of a community-oriented social enterprise in Gujarat/Subrata Dutta and Munish Alagh.
pages cm
Includes bibliographical references.
ISBN 9789332704275

1. Hearty Mart (Retail store). 2. Supermarkets--India--Gujarat. 3. Social entrepreneurship--India--Gujarat. 4. Rural development--India--Gujarat. I. Alagh, Munish, author. II. Title.

HF5429.215.I4D88 2017 DDC 381.149095475 23

Typeset, Printed and bound by The Book Mint, New Delhi.
www.thebookmint.in

CONTENTS

LIST OF TABLES AND FIGURES

TABLES

FIGURES

Foreword

It is often emphasised that rural Indian scene is rigid and slow in catching up with the changing times. This documentation of the rural India business dynamics has proved this wrong. The story of the evolution and growth of the 'Hearty Mart' in the state of Gujarat is an eye opener to the investors, marketers and business developers; and points to the beginning of the golden age of retail business in rural India.

'Business organisations' are increasingly realising the value of networking and trust as factors for enhancing economic value. 'Social entrepreneurship' is not so much appreciated mainly due to complexities and failure of the micro-financing institutions. Yet a genuine urge towards Social entrepreneurship emerged from community incorporated traditional and behavioural traits informalising a business model that has not only worked but thriving and expanding with decent levels of profits; in spite of multiple completions from within and outside the system.

This book is a record of the 'community franchising mechanism' in 'fast moving goods' including groceries. Both the sellers and buyers bear witness to traditional and conservative but rational groups who struggled within the realm of uncertainty; yet succeeded. The scenario that emerges is of a community fighting both for and against its own-self in being equal citizens of an emerging India. Mr Nadim Jafri, a self-made 'community entrepreneurial' leader of the Chiliyas—an intrepid business community of Gujarat—makes for an interesting case study of the Indian experiment in 'cultural diversity and economic progress' within the constraints and paradoxes which make the idea of india.

This book makes a compelling reading for those who are desirous of understanding the power of diversity, grit, devotion and business in bringing progress in the Indian economic development. Investors, business development strategists, academicians, media and the governments will benefit immensely from this book.

—Abusaleh Shariff, Ph.D
Chief Scholar and Mentor
US-India Policy Institute,
Washington D.C., USA

Acknowledgements

This study involves an investigation of a case of a 'community oriented' supermarket in Juhapura (Ahmedabad), namely Hearty Mart (which is led by the entrepreneur Nadeem Jafri who belongs to the family of the Syed Jafri, sect-head of the Shia Momin/Chilea community), and its rural franchising network across Gujarat. During the course of this research study, it has been a great opportunity for us to understand and analyse the social, organisational and other relevant aspects of this enterprise, and its franchising model.

At the outset, we would like to thank Indian Council of Social Science Research (ICSSR), New Delhi, for their financial support to this research project. Without their support, this book would not have come into existence. This study draws on the research infrastructure of our institute, namely Sardar Patel Institute of Economic and Social Research (SPIESR). We have received help and assistance from the staff members of our institute and their cooperation is gratefully acknowledged.

Our indebtedness to Nadeem Jafri, the main architect of Hearty Mart, and his colleagues cannot be properly expressed in words. We have been in touch with them quite frequently for various practical purposes and they have happily extended their help to us, without which it would not have been possible to carry out this study. We are extremely grateful to Dr Y.K. Alagh, Vice-Chairman and Professor Emeritus, SPIESR, and Chancellor, Central University of Gujarat (CUG) for his encouragement, inspiration and support for the present study. We thank Dr Abusaleh Shariff for kindly writing the Foreword for this book. We are also thankful to Dr Niti Mehta, Acting Director, SPIESR, for her support during this study.

We are grateful to two ICSSR-nominated advisors for this project—Dr Dinesh Awasthi, former Director and Professor, Entrepreneurship Development Institute of India (EDI), Gandhinagar, Gujarat, and Dr C.N. Ray, Professor, Centre for Environmental Planning and Technology (CEPT) University, Ahmedabad, Gujarat, for their useful comments on all the chapters. Their comments have helped us in improving the book. However, we bear the responsibility for the remaining errors, if any. We would also like to thank Kalki Soni, Pooja Bhatia, Mukesh Lakum, Pratap Chandra Bandhopadhya and Shri Ashwin Rawal for their research assistance.

—Subrata Dutta and Munish Alagh

1

Introduction

Background

Supermarkets are currently very popular shopping centres in urban India. It has been noted that the supermarkets are mainly located in cities and big towns. The concerned companies are reluctant to promote supermarket franchise in rural areas due to the fact that considerable section of the people in rural India has relatively low income and consequently has low purchasing power. Thus, access of rural people to modern shopping centres is limited. It is not clear how the gap between rural customers' desire to visit a supermarket on the one hand and big companies' reluctance to open and run supermarkets in rural areas on the others can be mitigated. In this study, we are concerned with a community-oriented business network which is functioning as retail/supermarket franchising enterprise in the state of Gujarat (mainly in rural area). The franchiser is located in the city of Ahmedabad whereas the franchisees are located in villages and small rural growth centres of different districts. The network is functioning under the banner of 'Hearty Mart' with two dimensions attached with it—one, the organisational aspects of a small-scale supermarket chain and, two, the concept of social entrepreneurship that has something to do with the people staying at bottom of the pyramid. Through such activities in rural areas, new employment opportunities may also be created. The geographical aspect is also important in this connection. For example, if some franchise retail store is found to be located in such areas where there were no other retail stores earlier, the local people are likely to benefit from such venture. Thus, Hearty Mart has strong bond with local areas in the sense that local community benefits from it in several ways (e.g.

entrepreneurship development, employment, accessibility of local rural people to retail outlet, low price, good quality items, etc.). The Hearty Mart organisation is the brainchild of Nadeem Jafri, the franchiser-entrepreneur, who first founded a supermarket in Juhapura area in Ahmedabad in 2004. He belongs to the family of the Syed Jafri sect head of the Shia Momin community. His religious superior position in his community has given him an opportunity to build a 'community-oriented' franchising network (i.e. a network that has engaged his community people as franchisees) of the Hearty Mart supermarket chain, since he has been able to persuade some enterprising persons of his own sect to start a franchise of Hearty Mart.

Some Relevant Issues

Generally, rigid contract terms are imposed on the franchisees by the franchiser as far as the 'formal' relation between them is concerned. In the case of Hearty Mart, the franchiser deals with village-level franchisees, most of whom have traditional mindsets and perhaps do not have adequate education. Thus, very formal relationship might not properly work in such business networks. Opening supermarket-type retail stores in Indian villages is a new idea. Hence, it may be argued that when a franchiser is initiating a new idea and dealing with village entrepreneurs, there is a need to adopt flexible contract terms, limited hierarchical authority, inspirational type of supervision, etc. But we are not sure about what kind of mechanism is being followed in the Hearty Mart system. This study seeks to look into this aspect of Hearty Mart business networks.

Social enterprise often links economic activities with social and community benefits through an organisational intervention. Organisation may play a crucial role in a situation where a community-oriented social enterprise is formed. This study, as said above, is concerned with franchising network of Hearty Mart. A franchising network also needs good organisational foundation, without which franchising business might face various constraints such as problem related to circulation of information within the networks, problem of coordination, high transaction cost, etc. The study of organisation emphasises the franchising process within a given framework. Also, emphasis is given to understand the complexity and various dimensions of a network-based organisation (including franchising networks).

Institutional trust assumes a special importance in the Hearty Mart model. A network-based organisational structure that considerably draws on institutional trust might have an advantage of exercising smooth functioning. Since most of the franchisees belong to the same religious sect in which the franchiser takes a higher position, there is a possibility that the parties involved in the activities can proceed forward with some trust that is embedded within religious bonding. Can such bonding be defined as formal? Perhaps not, since such bonding does not draw upon any formal contract. However, informal bonding may generate from religious fraternity of a community, which can often be seen as an institutional relationship. In such case, the formal institutional relationship based on legal contracts may not be found necessary, especially when most of the parties involved in the network are rooted in pastoral life with very limited education. In this context, it is imperative to look into the matters related to decision-making process (whether centralised, or decentralised, or both), contracts (whether formal or informal), the issue of property rights, the issue of flexibility or rigidity, motivation and innovation, among other things.

Apart from all this, the study seeks to understand whether the Hearty Mart model belongs to social enterprise. We need to examine whether the village-level entrepreneurs who are running their franchise retail stores are mostly from LIG (low-income group). Also, we need to examine whether a majority of the rural customers are from LIG and whether they are now getting access to supermarket-style shopping facility in their own locality (where the formal supermarket companies would not be generally interested in setting up any store). We need to investigate if the Hearty Mart supermarkets are selling high quality goods at relatively low prices. If so, it is expected that the local low-income customers are benefitting from the Hearty Mart stores. Hence, there is a possibility that such enterprises are catering to the needs of the rural poor in several ways. However, as said, there is a need to undertake an investigation of these aspects of such model, since the model is very unique in nature in the Indian context.

Objectives of the Study

With the brief introduction given above, we would now like to present the objectives of the study on the Hearty Mart supermarket franchising model.

- To understand about how in a complex external environment, a community develops a franchisee business model based on its own cultural institutional network.
- To investigate how a franchising network can be developed without formal/legal contracts and other stringent conditions between the parties involved.
- To examine whether or not a supermarket model can find growth trajectory in rural areas.
- To examine the organisational aspects of the model on the one hand and the social aspects of the model on the other.
- To know the views of the local customers about this rural supermarket model, especially in the context of the concept of social entrepreneurship. To look into the matter from the perspective of generation of livelihood for the rural people (both as franchisees and as employees).

Method of Investigation

In this study, we have adopted qualitative as well as descriptive methods of investigation. As indicated above, we have looked into the Hearty Mart model from the perspectives of organisational-institutional aspects and social entrepreneurship aspects. In order to understand the process of the development of the supermarket franchising model, all the parties—i.e. the franchiser and the franchisees—have been interviewed. Before the interview, we prepared two separate set of questionnaires—one is for the franchiser and the other for the franchisees. However, the interviews with them were not necessarily restricted to the questionnaires only because the questions we posed were not seeking objective answers. We knew that answer given by the respondent to one specific question might generate some other new questions that are difficult to be anticipated beforehand. Hence, there were scopes for exploring new relevant questions during the interview. Therefore, the interviews composed of both some predetermined questions and some exploratory questions. This has helped us to undertake a detailed qualitative analysis of the data and information.

As far as customers are concerned, we have adopted a bit different approach. Customers were not expected to give us elaborated answers in a short time of interview. For them, we prepared an objective type of questionnaire in a structured manner. An important reason for preparing such type of questionnaire was that we wanted to proceed for a tabular presentation of the data collected from the customers of Hearty Mart. As regards customer data collection, we have further elaborated the data collection procedure in Chapter 7. The analysis of the data followed descriptive approach and this has been done through presentations of various tables.

We think it is not useful to carry out some field survey in the surrounding areas of the location of the franchiser; rather, as said above, talking to the franchiser and the franchisees, on the one hand, and interviewing the samples of the customers, on the other, might be useful to understand this franchising business model and its objectives in a better way.

Chapter Organisation

In chapter 2, we describe in detail the whole structure of Hearty Mart organisation and the system within which its various segments operate. We elaborately describe the relation between the franchiser and the franchisees, and the role of intermediary sub-organisation in between them. An attempt has been made in this chapter to understand the supply-chain mechanism that is operating within the Hearty Mart model. The contribution of each segment of Hearty Mart from the perspective of value chain has also been exposed in chapter 2.

A detailed literature review has been done in chapter 3 in relation to the concepts of social entrepreneurship and Islamic views of entrepreneurship. Different features of social entrepreneurship have been presented in the chapter. Based on a conceptual model of social entrepreneurship, as formulated by Awasthi (2010), we have attempted to relate the model with the Hearty Mart in the context of "Bottom of the Pyramid" approach, creation of social values, financial self-sufficiency, clients' accessibility as well as affordability, and scalability, among others. We have also tried to review a question whether or not Islamic ethics have anything to do with (social) entrepreneurship. We wanted to review this question because this study is concerned with a franchising model that engages many people from the Islamic community (mainly the Chilea sect in the Shia-Momin community).

In chapter 4, various concepts that are relevant to the discussion of organisational economics, which further helps us in understanding a community-oriented franchising supermarket model, have been elaborately discussed. Understanding the concept of 'organisation' is useful to understand a community-based franchising model. That is why we have presented a detailed review of literature on the topics of organisational mechanism that consists of coordination and motivation, hybrid form of organisation, contractual responses to bounded rationality, property rights, and transaction costs, among many others.

In chapter 5, we empirically analyse the Hearty Mart model from the perspective of the social enterprise. This incorporates qualitative analysis of the primary information and data collected through field survey. The case study analysis shows that Hearty Mart with its religious ethics and bond has remained successful in serving the bottom of the pyramid in the local society. More importantly, Hearty Mart is not an organisation which can be regarded as a charitable trust; it is not engaged in any type of philanthropy or charity. Rather, it has been following market principles and (reasonable) profit-seeking objective. Most of the Hearty Mart retail stores are geographically located in far remote areas, and they are economically affordable for lower and middle class customers of rural areas. It has been offering different types of products of a range of wide varieties to rural customers.

Chapter 6 empirically elaborates different facets of organisational structure of Hearty Mart. It discusses the issues of property rights in connection with the village-based franchisees. The chapter investigates whether or not the relationship between franchiser and franchisees is healthy and well established in spite of absence of any formal deed of property rights. It studies whether religious trust and respect are the major components of property rights in the case of Hearty Mart and whether trust helps reduce transaction costs in business dealings within the organisation. The chapter digs into the matter, among many other issues, whether Hearty Mart follows centralised decision-making process, or decentralised decision-making process, or both. It also raises a question: can organisation solve many problems if some basic requirements of the local entrepreneurs (i.e. franchisees), e.g. level of education of the franchisees, are found to be inadequate.

Chapter 7 focuses on customers' views to assess the fact about how far the Hearty Mart has remained successful in achieving its social goals with a view to providing various opportunities to the local customers with limited means.

The book finally concludes with chapter 8, which provides a very brief overview of Hearty Mart and a summary of the important findings.

2

The Structure of Hearty Mart

Introduction

Hearty Mart is a franchising organisation which involves Juhapura-based franchiser, on the one hand, and village-level franchisees, on the other. However, the operational aspects of this franchising system involve various activities by several segments of its franchising chains. In this chapter, we try to understand them in a comprehensive manner. Especially, as far as a franchising system is concerned, there is a need to understand several important aspects—such as logistics, warehousing, distribution etc.—of the system. Before we proceed further to the next chapter, it is imperative to capture the whole structure and operational framework of the Hearty Mart Franchising system.

The Entities in Hearty Mart System

As said, to understand the entire structure of the Hearty Mart system, it is important for us to know the different segments involved in the franchising system and their respective functions. There are three major entities that are involved in the Hearty Mart system (Alagh 2008, Alagh and Christie 2011a). They are:

1) The Hearty Mart Supermarket at Juhapura (the franchiser).
2) The Hearty Mart Enterprise (HME).
3) The Hearty Mart Franchisee.

Each of them plays important role in the growth of this franchising business. Let us now go into details of each of these three entities.

The Hearty Mart Supermarket at Juhapura

The Hearty Mart Supermarket at Juhapura was established by Nadeem Jafri, the entrepreneur-franchiser, in the year 2004. As far as Hearty Mart larger organisation is concerned, it was the first venture of Nadeem within the organisation. Later, 'Hearty Mart' became a brand (Trivedi and Jafri 2008) and, in addition, Hearty Mart Juhapura became the parent body for the entire franchising chain or system. The process of development of this brand helped him to enter into the franchising venture (Narayanan 2012), tying up business linkages with the district level (or village level) franchisees. Thus, the Juhapura-based unit appeared as a franchiser in the Hearty Mart franchising network system which is explained later in further detail. The supermarket is basically engaged in sale of grocery items, foodgrains, cosmetics and some other domestic consumable items. The store, namely Hearty Mart Supermarket, itself is registered as an independent company, under the proprietorship of Nadeem Jafri. The supermarket occupies an area of 700 sq ft. But, the present space, as it seems, is limited as far as a supermarket store is concerned. However, with the growth of the business in the future, they may have to enhance the space (Alagh and Christie 2009a). There is a manager in Hearty Mart who handles the key functioning—i.e. from handling the staff and taking care of the books and cash register. The supermarket has 10 employees who take care of the different sections in the store. The Hearty Mart Supermarket at Juhapura is also the main office of the FDC (franchisee development cell) which we describe later in this chapter. The role of Nadeem in the supermarket is of a mentor, whereas the day-to-day decisions and management of the store are taken care of by the manager.

The Hearty Mart Enterprise

The HME is a company which is acting like a warehousing-cum-transportation unit for the larger Hearty Mart franchising organisation. It is an important component of the entire Hearty Mart System, which provides them with an opportunity to buy goods in bulk. For example, they can purchase items such as rice, pulses and spices, among many others, and store them in their own warehouse. This gives the company two benefits: 1) price benefit on bulk purchase, and 2) arbitrage benefit on pricing of commodities. The HME is also a company which is acting like an Enterprise of Private Label Goods of Hearty Mart's own creation. For example, the enterprise is engaged in activities related to food packaging and marketing the same. Earlier, this company had been originally owned by two partners Wajir Ali and Hussain Abbas in the name of Ashish Enterprises. In 2008, Nadeem joined this company as a partner. With the entry of Nadeem, Ashish Enterprise was converted into HME. Currently, there are four partners in this company. They are Nadeem Jafri, Wajir Ali, Mohammed Bhai, and Hussain Abbas, with equity share of 36 per cent, 21 per cent, 21 per cent, and 21 per cent, respectively. Of the total profit, 1 per cent goes to social development of the local area (Wajir Ali has been assigned by the company as the chief of it).

Why did Nadeem take initiative to form HME? As already indicated above, arbitrage of market prices at different points in time and in different places was one of his considerations. Also, providing goods of own brands to Hearty Mart franchisees and related stores and other organisations like restaurants was another motivation. While tying up with the franchisees in different villages, Nadeem felt it is important to provide their own private label merchandise to the franchisees at a reasonable rate (Alagh and Christie 2009b). Therefore, HME plays an important role in the supply-chain of the Hearty Mart franchising business (described later in further detail). However, here, we need to emphasise, in short, the need to look for additional market outlets as well, for the items warehoused in HME. Actually, the number of franchisees is not too large to create adequate demand for HME items. To properly manage the inventory, and, at the same time, to maintain the viability of the HME, there has been a need to look for additional market which they have been able to find in the restaurant chains run by the entrepreneurs of their own community, i.e. Shia/Chilea community. Nadeem being a member of the family of the sect-head of the Shia-Chilea community has been able to develop good links with the community living in different districts, and such links have in turn helped him to build business relationships with the Chilea restaurants (alongside the franchisee owners). Currently, HME acts as a major supplier for over 100 restaurants in and around Ahmedabad, and 300 restaurants across Gujarat. Nadeem developed the idea of such market extension for HME goods when he had come in contact with a small-scale supplier, namely Mukhi Sales which was owned by Mohammad Bhai. Mohammad Bhai used to supply products to some 50 Chilea restaurants. Nadeem offered him 20 per cent share in the HME and made him the partner in his supply company. This consolidation not only helped him to capture the restaurant supply chain of Mohammad Bhai, but also he has been successful in extending his supply business to a much larger number of restaurants across Gujarat. In the entire Hearty Mart System, the HME is the first preferred supplier to all the Hearty Mart Franchisees and the hotels/restaurants.

Let us now understand different activities that are done under the umbrella of HME. HME, as introduced above, is itself involved in processing of spices. In addition, they are involved in sale of foodgrains and sauces processing of which is outsourced. These products are sold under the brand names of 'Hearty Mart Good Time' (for dry-fruits and whole grain spices), 'Chef ki Pasand' (for spices),[1] and 'Hearty Mart' (for foodgrains). Thus, HME keeps creating new brands for which they receive all the necessary instructions and advices from Hearty Mart Juhapura unit and often via the corporate group. For the support, HME pays some royalty to Hearty Mart Juhapura unit. HME has three other associated companies under its umbrella. All activities of these companies are managed by HME.

The three associated companies or sub-organisations (which also pay royalty to the Hearty Mart Juhapura unit for all the support they

1. (a) Dry fruits such as almond, *chirongi/charauli*, whole cashews, cashew two pieces, cashew four pieces, poppy seeds, sesame seeds, black sesame seeds; and (b) spices such as carom seeds, star anise, whole coriander, green cardamom, *elaichi* white, dry rose leaf, whole asafoetida, nutmeg, mace, cumin seed, clove, black pepper, whole fenugreek, mustard seeds, cinnamon, bay leaf, fennel, etc.

receive from the Juhapura unit) under the broader umbrella of HME are briefly described below:[2]

1) Hearty Mart Logistics: It is a separate supply chain company which transports the merchandise from HME to franchisees and restaurants. It is owned by Baqar Ali.
2) Hearty Mart Celesta: It is a separate company within the HME which is involved in supplies of silver foil, plastic containers and lunch pack trays. These items are supplied to Chilea hotels and franchisees. Paper napkins and other packaging items are also supplied. They are provided under the brand Celesta or Hearty Mart itself. The company is owned by Abid Ali.
3) Hearty Mart Tea Packers: It is a separate company within the HME which is involved in processing and packaging of tea. They have two products called as 'Day Break Tea' and 'Adarsh Tea'. This company is owned by Sabbir Ali.

The Hearty Mart Franchisees

The Hearty Mart franchisees in villages are supermarkets and provisional stores which run under the banner of Hearty Mart. Each franchisee is registered as an independent company and is engaged with the Hearty Mart System under a simple contract involving 1) a franchisee fee (for one time only) and 2) refundable deposit for one year (see Table 2.1), as decided by the Hearty Mart parent organisation (i.e. the franchiser). After the first year of the contract, the franchisees move to a new contract where they are required to pay 0.5 per cent of their profits to the franchiser. This is a monthly fee in the form of royalty for the brand name of 'Hearty Mart'. We describe the relation between the franchiser and franchisee further in this chapter. Like the franchiser, the franchisees are also involved in selling of foodgrains, cosmetics, grocery and other domestic consumable items on retail basis. There are around four franchisees

2. HME is owned by two partners Nadeem Jafri and Wajir Ali. However, only Wajir has stake in the three associated companies, and Nadeem is not directly associated with them. But, Nadeem's Hearty Mart Juhapura unit receives some royalty from these three companies because they use Hearty Mart's brand name and also receives some support from the Juhapura unit.

which are supermarkets with space of around 600 sq ft to 1500 sq ft and seven provisional stores called as 'Saral Shops' with space of minimum 400 sq ft. The space or size of the shop is decided/ suggested as per the business potential of the locality which is estimated by both franchisee and franchiser.

Table 2.1

Franchisee Categories

Requirement	*440 Model*	*Super Store*	*Maxi Store*	*Tiny Store (Saral Shops)*
Required Store Space	Min 1500 sq ft	Min 800 sq ft	Min 600 Sq ft	Min. 400 Sq ft
Franchise Fees (in ₹)	75,440	55,440	35,440	25,440
Refundable Deposit (in ₹)	1,00,000	50,000	35,000	25,000
Investment (in lakh)	22-25 (excluding land)	13 (excluding land)	9.5 (excluding land)	7 (excluding land)

Source: *http://www.heartymart.com/index.php/our-business/retail* (see "Franchisee Structure" in this website)

Inferences about the Overall Structure of the Organisation

Initiating cooperation among business entities results in the formation of a sound organisational network, such as a franchising network. Theoretically, this has been well emphasised by Turek (2007). Obviously, not every instance of cooperation has led to such a result. It rather takes place in cases where several business entities cooperate with each other. One of these entities, in our case, the Hearty Mart Juhapura (i.e. the franchiser) is given a superior role, and it coordinates with the other entities (i.e. the ones that are involved in the network) in the matters of transfer of information and several other services.

The Three Entities and their Interrelationships

As described above, there are three entities within the larger Hearty Mart organisation. We have already described these entities individually. Let us now explain the relationships between them in detail.

The Hearty Mart Supermarket at Juhapura and Hearty Mart Franchisees

As already said, the Hearty Mart Supermarket at Juhapura, which is the franchiser, has established franchising networks with several franchisees across the state. Through this relationship, the franchisees are allowed to use the 'Hearty Mart' brand and, in exchange, the franchisees are liable to pay franchisee fees to the franchiser. In addition, the franchiser takes some responsibilities to promote business of its franchisees through its FDC. The FDC provides all the franchisees with necessary guidance and support in order to develop the village level supermarkets or Saral Shops of proper standard as has been set by the franchiser. The guidance and support include providing ideas about product packaging, presentation of the store, management of inventory and accounts management. Additionally, being a part of the Hearty Mart system, the franchisee gets access to the services of HME, which will be explained later in this chapter. In Figure 2.1, we have shown the relationship between the Hearty Mart Supermarket at Juhapura and Hearty Mart franchisees.

Figure 2.1

Relation between Hearty Mart Supermarket at Juhapura and Hearty Mart Franchisees

Source: Based on interview with the franchiser

In this respect, let us not forget to mention that the underlying foundation of such bonding between the franchiser and franchisees has something to do with their religious connection. As indicated earlier, a common thing observed among all the franchisees is that they all belong to the Chilea community.[3] Although being a Chilea is not a mandatory requirement to become a franchisee of the Hearty

3. The Chileas are a sect of Shia Muslims and they are very much business oriented and have entrepreneurial attitudes. Since Nadeem is a member of the sect-head family, the formation of the association has been easily possible.

Mart, the Hearty Mart franchising, however, has been possible for the direct involvement of some entrepreneurs of this particular sect. The franchiser-entrepreneur, Nadeem Jafri, who himself belongs to the sect-head of this community facilitated this network development. One big advantage of building such religion—or community-based network is that adequate trust which is an important component of any business relationship is generally thought to be present between the agents.

The Hearty Mart Supermarket at Juhapura and Hearty Mart Enterprise

To understand the relation between Hearty Mart Supermarket at Juhapura and HME, it is important to take note of the need for which the HME was formed. As a retailer, one has to deal with a lot of suppliers and also depend on them to obtain materials. The Hearty Mart Supermarket at Juhapura had faced some issues from suppliers mainly because of the fact that the suppliers were a bit reluctant to supply goods to Juhapura due to some social reasons (Thaker 2008, Zahir 2013). Thus, to reduce dependence on the suppliers, the HME was founded which has been giving the opportunity to the concerned stakeholders within the Hearty Mart System to buy goods in bulk and, thus, has helped them to maintain a certain degree of economies of scale. Hence, HME is found to have acted as a super-stockist which warehouses and transports goods to the Hearty Mart Supermarket at Juhapura and all its franchisees in villages as and when they are needed in desirable quantities (in other words, HME can be termed as a producer-cum-distributor of Hearty Mart's own branded private label goods). The HME is located at Juhapura and such locational proximity between the franchiser and the stockist facilitates easy coordination.

The Hearty Mart Enterprise and the Hearty Mart Franchisees

Let us now elaborate further the relationship between HME and Hearty Mart Franchisees. As we have already seen, the franchiser-entrepreneur of the Hearty Mart organisation believes in a business policy of 'having one's own stockist' while running a franchising business. As we have also indicated, the role of a stockist is very important in any franchising business. However, it is particularly important in the Hearty Mart franchising business. Why is it 'particularly' important? But all the Hearty Mart Franchisees are located in villages, while some are even located in remote villages. Timely availability of goods in remote villages is instrumental for a franchisee in order to cater to its customers on a regular basis (Talukdar 2009). Thus, uninterrupted functioning of franchising business is something which relates to the reputation of a growing brand. Also, having one's own set of branded products such as sauces, tea, etc. is important too. Such type of business value seems to be contributing—in whatever small way—to the growth of modern India, a concept which often relates to urban India and in most cases excludes rural India (Trivedi 2009). But, the concept of modern India should include both village and cities.

However, in the Hearty Mart system, there is no compulsion for a franchisee on hiring HME as a supplier. A franchisee can utilise any supplier it wishes to hire. But, a close tie between HME and franchisees may bring about higher growth for the entire Hearty Mart organisation, because, through this relationship, the products that are manufactured/packaged by the HME itself can find an outlet through the channels of their own system. In a way, it is a kind of promotional initiative which engages different sister organisations within a larger organisation system through cooperation between each other in the interest of the larger system.

The Hearty Mart System

In this section, we try to study the interrelationships among the entities of the Hearty Mart System. If we integrate them, we get an overall illustration of the whole structural framework (as shown in Figure 2.2). The linkages between the franchiser and the franchisee, between the franchiser and HME, and between HME and franchisee have been clearly described above. So, they do not require any further elaboration.

Figure 2.2

The Entire Hearty Mart System

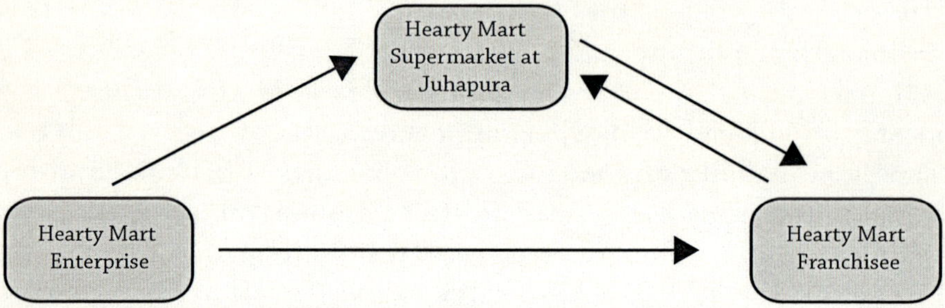

Source: Based on interview with the franchiser.

Inferences about the Relation between the Entities

Franchising enterprises are often referred to as 'franchise network' or 'franchise system.' There are various types of relations among the different entities in the network. In the case of Hearty Mart, involvement in similar line of business, say groceries, has helped in building the network between the different entities such as the franchiser, franchisees and the intermediate organisation. This has, in turn, resulted in enrichment of individual business entities involved and increase in their efficiency as far as the utilisation of their resources/capabilities and specialisations is concerned. Network connections can also be created among companies/entities that have complementary lines of business. Say, for instance, Hearty Mart Juhapura is engaged in the sale of grocery and consumable items and HME is engaged in the supply/distribution of spices, pulses, etc., on the one hand, and is also engaged in storage and packaging, on the other. This results in a comprehensive operational system which often helps an organisation or a network in gaining a better position in the market.

Within the framework of the Hearty Mart franchising system, the Juhapura unit plays the central role and coordinates different functions in the network. The subordinate entities (i.e. Hearty Mart franchisees) retain their autonomy as far as daily operations are concerned, but have to follow directions and standards imposed on them by the superior entity (Hearty Mart Juhapura). From the formal viewpoint, the interdependence actually exists only between the franchiser and the franchisee. Individual franchisees are independent of one another, since there takes place no exchange of resources among them. Of course, franchisee entities exchange information in the meetings organised by the coordinator. However, as already indicated, the network coordinator plays the most important role in formulating strategies, specifying the ways of utilising resources, establishing norms, and so on. Subordinate entities which enter the franchise system are informed about all necessary details of its functioning.

Monitoring of the Integrated System

In the offset of an organised effort to make so many sub-organisations work together in a system, it was important to establish a core group in order to monitor the system for its smooth functioning. The reason was that there was a need to establish a management mechanism which could help in understanding the upcoming issues and taking necessary steps for further improvement. For this purpose, in early 2014, they have made an informal group, called as the Hearty Mart Corporate Group, incorporating Hearty Mart Supermarket, HME, and FDC to discuss emerging issues and required measures. It helps to track information and activities that are related to day-to-day work, on the one hand, and each level of the system, on the other.

In the above-mentioned core group, the FDC plays a very important role since it maintains close relationships with all the Hearty Mart Franchisees. The FDC provides updated information, about the development, including the sales of all the franchisees and reports the details to the Hearty Mart Corporate Group. Here, the executive-in-charge of the FDC is responsible for these activities. In this regard, all the data analysis work is done by an analyst who handles the tracking of sales, accounting and other related activities. There is also an executive in FDC, who keeps an eye on the overall developments in the market from time to time and informs the same to the monitoring group, and finally passes on the advices of the group to the franchisees for further development of the retail units.

The Value Chain Model and the Hearty Mart System

We not only need to understand the structure of the organisation but also the activities that flow in and around the structure. We describe it in the form of value chain model (see Figure 2.3) which was developed by Michael Porter (1988). A value chain is the set of activities that a company performs to deliver a product or service to the market. We will explain the entire Hearty Mart Value Chain in two parts:

1) Primary Activities: This includes activities such as inbound logistics, operations, outbound logistics, marketing and sales, and services.
2) Support System: This includes amenities and activities such as firm infrastructure, human resource management, technological development, and procurement.

We now explain each of them individually in the context of the Hearty Mart System.

Figure 2.3

The Value Chain Model

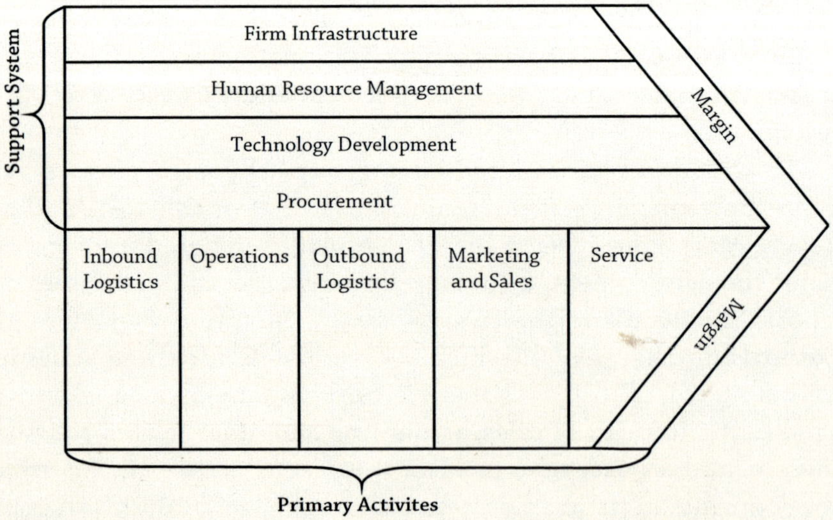

Source: Porter (1988).

Primary Activities

Inbound Logistics: The activities that fall under the inbound logistics are material collection and procurement. The logistics is the medium of transport of the goods and accordingly it provides services to the Hearty Mart Supermarket at Juhapura and its franchisees. Having its own logistics set-up in the Hearty Mart system makes the company self-sufficient since it has been free from dependence on external agency for the said purpose. What types of products does the Hearty Mart Logistics procure? The products such as spices, rice, tea, silver foils, etc., are procured from the mills or the suppliers in bulk. The franchiser warehouses these materials in the HME in large quantities so that supply of goods to the marketing outlets remains uninterrupted at every point in time.

Operations: As far as some intermediary operations are concerned, the HME and associated accompanies (Hearty Mart Tea, Celesta, Chef ki Pasand, etc.) are responsible for packaging all their goods under their respective brand labels and preparing the finished product. They have in-house set-ups for packaging each product and all the assembling takes place in the HME by their own staff and labour.

Outbound Logistics: The outbound logistics is managed primarily by the HME which collects orders from the hotels, restaurants and Hearty Mart Franchisees. After the orders are taken, the Hearty Mart Logistics takes care of the delivery of goods. For all the Hearty Mart Franchisees, this is a support system through which timely supply of goods is ensured.

Marketing and Sales: All the stakeholders such as the HME, franchiser and franchisees are involved in marketing. The pricing of the goods is taken care of by the HME. As said earlier, the retail sale activities are managed by both Hearty Mart franchisees and franchiser. In this regard, the additional role which is played by the HME includes supplying some goods (spices, foodgrains, foils, etc.) to the various restaurants/hotels run by Chilea community entrepreneurs who are not part of the Hearty Mart System.

Service: Since the grocery items are mainly marketed through the franchising system, there is hardly any need for after-sales services. However, as said earlier, the HME not only supplies its products to the franchisees, but it also supplies various products to different Chilea-run restaurants. There are some post-sales services that HME delivers to the restaurants by means of having interactions with the chefs regarding the use of products. For this purpose, the Hearty Mart organises seminars and training sessions at regular intervals.

Margin: All the primary activities are given horizontally in Figure 2.3 and each activity indicates a stage of the value chain. It is expected that each activity is contributing to better efficiency of the organisation and margin of profit. However, margin of profit is not only a function of primary activities, but also a function of support system. Let us now describe the support system in the Hearty Mart System.

Support System

Firm Infrastructure: Let us now consider the infrastructure part of the Hearty Mart System. In a broad sense, the HME and the Hearty Mart Retail (both Franchisees and the Franchiser) constitute the infrastructure of the Hearty Mart System. The HME is located at two places: 1) The first building which is the main centre is located at Juhapura. All the major activities of HME such as running the associated companies namely Hearty Mart Logistics, Hearty Mart Tea Packers, and Hearty Mart Celesta take place in the Juhapura premises (Alagh and Christie, 2011b). It serves as the major warehousing facility of the company. 2) The second extension of HME is located at Surat, which works as a major junction in the process of supply of goods to the hotels/restaurants on the Bombay-Surat route.

The Hearty Mart Franchisees are of four types as we have seen in Table 2.1, which gives us different features of the four types of franchisees.

Human Resource Management: The company runs with a principle that the Hearty Mart Franchisee is an independent firm which has gone for a partnership agreement with the franchiser on the basis of royalty system. Thus, there is no direct hierarchy between the franchiser and the franchisee as such. However, the franchiser, as indicated above, provides the franchisees with suggestions and advice through the FDC. The FDC guides all franchisees with various skills for product packaging, product positioning, arrangement of the store to place goods through correct methods for drawing attention of the customers, inventory analysis, preparation of accounts, maintenance of cash register, order analysis and sales forecasting, providing knowledge on execution of product schemes, customer handling and management of crowd in shop. In addition, the FDC also helps the franchisees in relation to security of the store and day-to-day execution of retail. Thus, the FDC is a corner stone of this franchising system in which it has been endeavouring to elevate all the franchisees to a greater scale of professional enthusiasm in order to expand and grow the retail ventures of the franchisees.

However, there exists a management-cum-staff structure in the Hearty Mart System and the structure is as follows:

1) Nadeem Jafri: Chief Mentor at Hearty Mart-He makes most of the policy decisions and looks into the various opportunities, as and when available in the market, to improve the value chain and the Heart Mart System.
2) Wazir Ali and Hussain Abbas: Partners and managers of the HME—They look into the daily activities like procurement and supply activities of the HME.

A few employees work for the smooth running of the management. They include an executive in charge of FDC, an analyst-cum-account, executives to manage the franchisees and supporting staff (such as people for loading and unloading goods, packaging, delivery etc).

Technology: As regards technology in the Hearty Mart system, the organisation has been working with simple components like a unit of packaging, and computers for accounting. However, there is a scope for introducing information technology in the Hearty Mart system in a far greater scale, especially in tracking the sales that take place at the franchisee-outlets and for tracking inventory at the store. Such tracking would enhance the level of transparency in the organisation system (especially, in the relationship between the franchiser and the franchisee) on the one hand; and thus greater marketing-related information would help the franchiser to identify the areas in which the franchisees need more training and assistance, on the other.

Procurement: This is a primary activity of HME which takes care of logistics and supplying all the franchisees and hotels/restaurants with necessary goods/items/inputs. Why is procurement of goods at favourable prices an important part of a value chain? The reason is that goods can be sold in reasonable price only when goods are procured at right prices. So procurement decisions and procurement accomplishments are instrumental for the growth of the organisation. There is scope for improving procurement system by introducing/ launching management information system, high-tech vehicles etc. in the organisation.

The support systems are shown vertically in Figure 2.3 with each system contributing to each primary activity at various levels. This complementary relationship between them may be found crucial for the growth of the organisation. The arrow on the right hand side of Figure 2.3 indicates that an integrated approach is required to drive an organisation towards forward direction.

Inferences

Hearty Mart marketing activities are by and large guided by the central store (i.e. the franchiser located at Juhapura). The central store takes into account individual marketing requirements of different regions and provides the pamphlets etc. Individual franchisees are responsible for specific store marketing beyond this. Procurement and distribution of goods is also taken care of by Hearty Mart Juhapura; and HME takes into account requirements of individual region (i.e. village-based individual franchisees). As far as expansion of franching operations are concerned, Hearty Mart does not intend to expand beyond its targeted area of north and central Gujarat. Employment of staff is responsibility of individual store. However training/guidance is constantly provided by the Hearty Mart FDC.

The advantages of functioning within a franchise network include reduction of risk, increased flexibility, an opportunity for acquiring new capacity for development, facilitated access to scarce sources and skills, increased speed of operation, facilitated acquisition of information, among others (Child and Faulkner,

1998). An opportunity of facilitated access to scarce resources and skills in network organisations appears due to the fact that the resources and skills of partners operating within such a network are complementary. However, the acquaintance of the franchisees with the local market is important. Also, the franchisees are responsible for the recruitment of staff to be employed in their outlets. It happens extremely rarely that employees for a specific outlet are recruited by the network coordinator. From the point of view of the franchisees, it is advantageous that the franchiser provides professional help and consulting to them. The results of any market research carried out by the headquarters become also available to the franchisees. The franchiser sometimes organises promotional and advertising campaigns for the franchisees. Furthermore, the network as a whole has a more powerful bargaining position, which means that it can negotiate with the concerned parties (e.g. dealer or distributor or manufacturer/producer) for better conditions for supply, preferential conditions for credit supply, among others. The employment structure of Hearty Mart Group reflects the fact so far that the organisation has grossly been interested in offering opportunities to the poor villagers. As far as the Hearty Mart Franchiser is concerned, the organisation has chosen a place called Sathal village in the outskirts of Ahmedabad city to employ 35 residents as the workers for their city-based activities. A free bus service is provided by the organisation for all the employees for their regular transport, something which would not have otherwise been provided by other employers.

The new network participant (i.e. a new franchisee) joins a structure whose effectiveness has already been proved, takes over standards that have proved to be correct (in the functioning of the Parent Hearty Mart), benefits from the recognised trademark, etc. Such a situation certainly involves less risk than starting a business activity on one's own. However, it has to be stressed once again that reduction of risk is possible only when the franchiser has an effective idea to offer, and it is not an attempt at rescuing their company by utilising the resources of franchisees. It happens very rarely that an idea which has not been tested on the market proves to be effective in franchise activity.

The acquired information ought to be complete and up-to-date, and conclusions drawn from the information ought to be utilised in due time. In network organisations information can be exchanged among the partners within the network. Cumulating resources that are utilised for research provides an opportunity for acquiring more complex data and a better interpretation of the acquired data. In companies operating within a franchise network, there can be differentiated three basic types of information flow: gathering information from market environment directly by the centre of the network, providing information on the local markets by particular entities involved in the network, and internal flow of information between the franchiser and franchisees, based on positive feedback. All this strengthens the functioning of the network.

3

Social Entrepreneurship and Islamic Views of Entrepreneurship

Introduction

The purpose of this chapter is to review the literature related to social entrepreneurship and Islamic entrepreneurship. Thus, in the first half of this chapter, we discuss the issues of social entrepreneurship, while the second half is devoted to Islamic entrepreneurship. Social entrepreneurship has been the subject of considerable interest in the literature of economic development. This phenomenon includes vast range of personal initiatives and social organisational structures (Roper and Cheney 2005). This can be explained as a process in which an entrepreneur initiates a project and brings together a number of members of a community. As in the case of Hearty Mart, the project takes place on the basis of 'personal initiative', involving its own community members in the organisation.

For any country, social entrepreneurship is very important for economic development because it creates social and economic values like employment, innovation (with regard to goods and services), social capital and equity. In this regard, Hearty Mart is seen to be an organisation which has created employment for the people of Shia Momin (Chelia community) and other communities in villages and rural small towns through its various types of organisations such as franchiser store, franchisee stores, Hearty Mart Enterprise (HME) and associated organisations. Secondly, initiating supermarket stores in villages is an innovative idea, through which people will have an opportunity to move, at least partly, from pastoral view to modern view. And, thirdly, bringing the Shia Momin community together through this venture reflects on the community social capital. Social entrepreneurship paves the way to a future that may allow coming generations to find their livelihoods (Seelos and Mair 2008). Social entrepreneurs are in search of innovative models that seek to help people in their surroundings to find betterment in life. Let us now discuss social entrepreneurship in detail in the light of the existing literature.

The Concept, Features and Perspectives of Social Entrepreneurship

In this section, based on the review of literature, we are going to discuss the concepts and various features of social entrepreneurship in detail.

The Concept of 'Social Entrepreneurship'

There is no scholarly consensus on the definition of the term 'social entrepreneurship'. The concept of social entrepreneurship means different things to different people and researchers (Dees 1998). Social entrepreneurship is generally conceptualised as a two sided entity, which includes 'social' and 'entrepreneurial' dimensions (Peredo and McLean 2006). Let us now elaborate this further. Systematic examination of the two defining terms of the concept, namely 'social' and 'entrepreneurship', allows us to capture the essence of social entrepreneurship and explore potential differences between social entrepreneurship and entrepreneurship in the business sector (Mair and Marti 2006).

In the 20th century, Joseph Schumpeter (1934) described entrepreneurs as the innovators who drive the process of 'creative destruction' in the development of capitalism. In his words: "An entrepreneur is an innovator who implements entrepreneurial change within markets." The entrepreneurial change has been described as the introduction of a new or improved good, the introduction of a new method of production, the opening of a new market, the exploitation of a new source of supply and the carrying out of the new organisation of any industry. Innovation or newness is the core characteristic of an entrepreneur in this definition. As

Audretsch (1995) notes, just as entrepreneurs are agents of change, entrepreneurship is about the process of change. As far as the Hearty Mart is concerned, indeed, change is inherent in this franchising model. As regards newness, prominent feature includes the mode of delivery through supermarkets in villages. In fact, Hearty Mart has introduced a new mode of shopping in villages, i.e. in hitherto isolated locations, through supermarkets that are manifested as organisations of the community identification. Cole (1949) explains entrepreneurship as a goal-oriented activity that initiates, maintains and develops profit-oriented venture through interaction with the surrounding economic, social and political circumstances. Hence, the conventional view refers to entrepreneurs as individuals who initiate change and innovation in the market and it is considered that their primary focus is to build business and earn profit.

A social entrepreneur, on the other hand, aims to serve communities and society, while generating profit for his company. The major factor that distinguishes social entrepreneurship from entrepreneurship is the motivation for bringing about social change (Mair and Marti 2006). According to Mair and Marti (2006), while private venture efforts to focus on earning profits and, hence, emphasises the development of economic value, social venture emphasises social value over economic value, maintaining a position that economic value creation is a necessary condition to ensure financial viability. Mair and Marti (2006) opine that social entrepreneurship is mainly viewed as an activity of social change, which promotes social values and improves the well-being of people involved in the process of enterprising (see also Nicholls 2008, Zahra et al. 2009).

Social Entrepreneurship: Different Features and Perspectives

The aim in the Hearty Mart System is both to improve the well-being of the franchisees and the customers and to impart social values which Nadeem's cousin who is the sect head underlines in his teachings. These are in fact defining elements of the venture. More specifically, we can say that until now, no supermarket group or franchisers in India have tried to cater to village customers by finding franchisees in villages, ignoring relatively unimpressive/adverse economies of scale attached to poor infrastructure and amenities in villages. However, there is a long-standing debate in the literature about different features and perspectives of social entrepreneurship. Let us now elaborate this.

Social entrepreneurship encompasses the notion of 'construction, evaluation and pursuit of opportunities' as a means for social change by the visionary, passionately dedicated individuals (Roberts and Woods 2005). According to Popoviciu and Popoviciu (2011), social entrepreneurship evolves based on the specific components of context, characteristics and outcomes. The context may relate to poverty, exclusion, inequality and/or marginalisation, while the characteristics are found in the direct action of passionate, committed and driven individuals, known as the social entrepreneurs. Social change is the actual outcome which can be either small-scale (i.e. very much local) or large-scale. A broader conceptualisation of different features of social entrepreneurship differs from one author to another. Trivedi (2010) features social entrepreneurship into four common themes: 1) focus on social profit rather than economic profit, 2) creating and using economic profit as a means of solving social problems rather than an end in itself, 3) elements of social innovation and entrepreneurship, and 4) the social activist's role played by the social entrepreneur.

In the view of Dees (1998), social entrepreneurship plays the role of change in the society by: 1) adopting a mission to create and sustain social value (not just private value), 2) recognising and relentlessly pursuing new opportunities to serve that mission, 3) engaging in a process of continuous innovation, adaptation and learning, 4) acting boldly without being limited by resources currently in hand, and 5) exhibiting heightened accountability to the constituencies served and for the outcomes created. A realisation that the existing set of resources must not be a limit on growth where resources are created through a chain of interacting processes is a precondition as far as establishing a social enterprise is concerned.

In a study, Zahra et al. (2009) explain the contribution of social entrepreneurship in creating social wealth. They noted that social entrepreneurship encompasses the activities and processes undertaken to discover, define and exploit opportunities in order to enhance social wealth by creating new venture or managing existing organisation in an innovative manner. Mair and Marti (2006) explain social entrepreneurship as a process of creating value by combining resources in new ways and, according to them, these resource combinations are intended primarily to explore and exploit opportunities to create social value and thus, to stimulate social change or meet social needs. Employing novel types of resources and combining them in new ways, social entrepreneurship is a rich field for the discovery of new models of value creation (Seelos and Mair 2008).

Zahra et al. (2009) examine social entrepreneurship from an entrepreneurial perspective based on the work of scholars who belong to the Austrian School of Economics such as Hayek, Kirzner and Schumpeter.[1] In their paper, they identify three types of social entrepreneurs: 1) Social Bricoleurs: acting upon local needs, being on the spot with the skills to address local problems not in the focus of others,[2] 2) Social Constructionists: acting in a more institutionalised perspective by addressing gaps in the provision of socially significant goods,[3] and 3) Social Engineers: embracing

---

1. The Austrian School is a school of economic thought that is based on methodological individualism. It originated in late 19th and early 20th century in Vienna with the work of Carl Menger, Eugen von Böhm-Bawerk, Friedrich von Wieser, and others. Current-day economists working in this tradition are located in many different countries, but their work is referred to as Austrian economics. Among the theoretical contributions of the early years of the Austrian school are the subjective theory of value, marginalism in price theory, and the formulation of the economic calculation problem, each of which has become an accepted part of mainstream economics.

   Many economists are critical of the current-day Austrian School and consider its rejection of econometrics and aggregate macroeconomic analysis to be outside of mainstream economic theory, or "heterodox."

2. Social Bricoleurs usually focus on discovering and addressing small-scale local social needs.

3. Social Constructionists typically exploit opportunities and market failures by filling gaps to underserved clients in order to introduce reforms and innovations to the broader social system.

innovation in a true Schumpeterian disruptive angle by seeking to change the social equilibrium.[4] Fowler (2000) has produced a complex social entrepreneurship typology, highlighting three categories of entrepreneurial social activities: 'integrated social entrepreneurship', 're-interpretation', and 'complementary social entrepreneurship'.

Features of social entrepreneurship have been reviewed by Peredo and McLean (2006). According to her, social entrepreneurship is enabled where some person or persons aim either exclusively or in some prominent way to create social value of some kind, and pursue that goal through some combination of: 1) recognising and exploiting opportunities to create this value, 2) employing innovation, 3) tolerating risk and 4) declining to accept limitations in available resources.

In Anna Maria's study, a further important point is that of innovative development as compared to the neo-classical Laissez Faire Avatar.[5] The classical concept of broad based development beyond the pockets of 'upper classes' dates back to the publications of Marx's volumes which elaborately deal with 'classes'. Socialist view of class doctrine fails to capture a secluded community's hopelessness. Even a socialist redistribution policy may not reach out to a particular group, if the policy making body does not take into account the concerns of all the sections of the society. In such kinds of market imperfections of a non-pareto efficient kind, broad based development may become difficult.

Social Entrepreneurship and Community Development

Social entrepreneurship arises from entrepreneurial activities with aim of achieving sustainable development of the community. Social entrepreneurship can be viewed as a bottom-up model of socio-economic development that seeks to overcome government and market failures (James 2010). Wallace (1999) examines the

4. Social engineers recognise systemic problems within existing social structures and address them by introducing revolutionary change.

5. Laissez-faire is a policy dictating a minimum of governmental interference in the economic affairs of individuals and society. It was promoted by the physiocrats and strongly supported by Adam Smith and John Stuart Mill.

role of social enterprise in facilitating community development. He noted that social entrepreneurs have social responsibility to improve their community which derives from social and political cohesion in a community leader. According to Nagler (2007), social entrepreneurship should take important place in economic development policies because it can play a vital role to the progress of societies and deliver vital value to societal and economic development. Social entrepreneurship plays an important role in sustainable development of the community. Hence, it is important to review the link between them, if a proposed study has left room for such review.

According to the report of the World Commission on Environment and Development (1987), sustainable development is the development that meets the needs of the present without compromising the ability of future generations to meet their own need. To implement this definition, the United Nations (UN) defined a set of Millennium Development Goals (MDGs), based on a resolution adopted by the General Assembly in September, 2000. In this context, Seelos and Mair (2008) state that social entrepreneurship creates new models for the provision of products and services that carter directly to the social needs underlying sustainable development goals such as the MDGs. Amina Omrane (2013) views social entrepreneurship as an assistance tool for the government and applied to the resolution of social problems. According to her, social entrepreneurship can provide an analysis framework in order to provide a response to the challenges of sustainable development. The author also showed the usefulness of the different business models developed in social entrepreneurship, particularly in the European context and conclude that social business models constitute a basic relay that allow social entrepreneurs to contribute actively to sustainable development. As regards social entrepreneurial ventures, Nicholls (2008) also explains the sustainability options. Bill Drayton (2002) considered social entrepreneurship to be the result of very special personal traits shared by only a small percentage of the population, traits that go beyond altruistic motivation and reflect a determination to change the whole of society. Salamzadeh et al. (2011) defines social entrepreneurship as a recurring process starting from social idea formation to gaining through some steps towards social values creation, which lead to social change and sustainable development. According to Alvord et al. (2004), social entrepreneurship creates innovative solutions to immediate social problems and mobilises the idea, capacities, resources and social arrangements required for sustainable social transformation. Nicholls (2008) argues that social entrepreneurship is a set of innovative and effective activities that focus strategically on resolving social market failures and creating new opportunities to add social value systematically by using a range of resources and organisational formats to maximise social impact and bring about changes.

Further, the core element which strengthens the link between social entrepreneurship and sustainable development of the community is its innovative character of initiative. Innovation may mean starting new organisation, or offering new products or services (Mair and Marti 2006). According to Peredo and McLean (2006), innovative ideas can be completely new inventions or creative adoptions of existing ones. Organisation for Economic Cooperation and Development (OECD 2011) describes innovation as a key source of long-term growth.

Social innovation is by nature multi-dimensional insofar as a variety of issues are addressed as social challenge, which entails a significant degree of diversity in terms of knowledge based on science and technology (OECD 2011). Drayton (2002) noted that "social entrepreneurs are not content just to give fish or teach how to fish. They will not rest until they have revolutionised the fishing industry." Like other entrepreneurs, social entrepreneurs are creative thinkers and continuously striving for innovation, which can involve new technologies, supply-sources, distribution outlets, or methods of production (Dees 1998).

From all these perspectives, social entrepreneurship can be described as innovative and sustainable solution to the social problems. According to Murphy and Coobes (2009), social entrepreneurship is often seen as the creation and undertaking of a venture, intended to promote a specific social purpose or cause.

However, to work for a social cause, passion is very important. In this regard, Dees (1998) argued that social entrepreneurship combines the passion of a social mission with an image of business-like discipline, innovation and determination. We describe this issue later again in terms of Awasthi's (2010) conceptualisation. Germak and Singh (2009) in their paper argued that, given the tremendous need for solution to today's pressing social challenges, it is time for social workers to stand up and embrace much of the straightforward business sense found in social entrepreneurship, a hybrid of social-work principles and business innovation activities. Such co-existence is possible, when business innovation activities are undertaken to promote a larger social cause, not just for fulfilling personal financial ambitions (Roy 2013). Mort et al. (2002) conceptualise social entrepreneurship as a multi-dimensional construct involving the expression of entrepreneurially virtuous behaviour to achieve the social mission, a coherent unity of purpose and action in the face of moral complexity, the ability to recognise social value creating opportunities, and key decision-making characteristics of innovativeness, proactiveness and risk-taking. Swanson and Zhang (2010) construct positions of social entrepreneurship based on their planned methods for implementing social change and the level of business practices they implement to do so. Social entrepreneurs have to be psychologically attuned to combat different obstacles. A growing number of initiatives all over the globe seem to be defying the obstacles that have prevented businesses from providing services to the poor (Seelos and Mair 2005). Nicholls and Cho (2008) have seen social entrepreneurship from the perspective of sociality, innovation and market orientation.

Some Salient Features of Social Entrepreneurship

According to Awasthi (2010), social entrepreneurship is primarily about the passion which drives certain individuals. It is a "passion to change the world, a passion to improve the way things were happening around." A social/community entrepreneur may not be a revolutionary, but he is motivated by change and desires to seek light for his community, initiate innovative as well as affordable products/

services, create sustainable employment opportunities, etc. Awasthi further states that social entrepreneurship is about the passion which certain individuals share towards bringing a sustainable social change, using a market-based model that does not bypass the poor instead, they treat the poor as valuable customers and consumers and not an object of their bounty. They follow 'best practices' to bring about 'next practices' and have vision to change—not the rules of the game but the game itself. The efficient and sustainable management practices and processes that such enterprises use are not based merely on creating social value. Products are often sold by them at lower than MRP, while quality of product is ensured.

A social enterprise model also reinforces that sensitivities are still alive and there are people who think beyond self and consider is that many things that have been happening are neither sustainable nor worth sustaining (UNDP *Human Development Report 1996*, cited in Awasthi, 2010). Indeed, a social/community entrepreneur realises that if a section of population is poor and deprived of many basic things of life, then the social development may not be sustainable. Thus, to correct the situation, development requires a sustainable and equitable model that thinks beyond self and beyond discrimination so that the society is not divided into privileged and unprivileged sections. Awasthi (2010) elaborates that when governments fail, markets are seldom able to enforce a corrective mechanism. Thus, market-based activities that have social views can undertake corrective measures.

Awasthi (2010) further writes using Schumpeter's 'innovation' framework that social entrepreneurship also brings in efficacy through product/service innovation, process innovation, market innovation, organisational innovation and innovation related to new source of material (see also Emerson and Economy 2001). It offers market-based solutions to social problems. It also challenges the market status quo by introducing new variety of organisational structures. One of the ways may be to connect villages through supply chains of new organisations and thus create new opportunities (both business and employment) in rural areas (Alagh and Bandhopadhya 2015).

Awasthi further quotes Alter (2006) who characterises social entrepreneurship as an ability to combine social interests with business practices to effect social change. Its hybrid world, part business and part social, has spawned a new breed of practitioners, the social entrepreneur, as well as a new brand of organisation, the revenue earning social enterprise (p.205). This definition emphasises the fact that a social entrepreneur does not miss out both the social objective and the objective of revenue earning. Such structure of organisation is different from other business organisation since the structure of a social enterprise seeks to accommodate a section of population that is lagging behind the privileged.

Winning Factors for Social Enterprises

As defined by Awasthi (2010: 6), "social enterprise is for-profit, socially relevant, innovative and sustainable economic activity that provides goods and services at an affordable price to people who are at the bottom of the pyramid. It brings goods and services within the reach, usability and affordability of the people who otherwise would find it difficult to access and afford." Based on organisational theories, he proposes the following key characteristics of sustainable social enterprises:

1) Addressing critical social and/or economic issues confronting Bottom of the Pyramid: Awasthi argues that social enterprises are mission-centric and issue-based depending upon the leanings of these promoters and would address some problems of the target group. In some areas, especially in villages, the community target group may not have access to affordable, convenient, fair (e.g. transparent billing system), reasonable, efficient service of supermarkets. Accessibility to quality product as well as branded product at local area is another concern. These gaps can be mitigated through new franchise model. Products can be provided at discounted rates or some products at most at MRP (since some retailers sell goods in villages at more than MRP). There is a need to create a retail format in villages that would satisfy the needs of all types of customers, not just the middle and upper-

middle class consumers. Credit facility for the poor should also be available in such format.

2) Innovative and creates social value: Product developments in social enterprises are based on a sound understanding of the operational aspects of the product; and the bottom line is that they ensure creation of social value, which is reflected in the improvement of the lives of the target people. In this regard, we may argue that selecting villages or rural small growth centres for organised retail/supermarket is a way forward. Employment creation in the locality is an important aspect. In addition, products need to be quality assured; they need to be stacked well; and they need to be priced correctly, among others.

3) Financial self-sufficiency: One of the important task is to have self-sustaining models, while, at the same time, they have a social view. But, the social view does not incorporate any idea of grant or subsidy; rather, this has to be accommodated within the viability strategies. Since, in a flexible franchising model, franchisees are at freedom to adopt their own pricing strategies, there may be a need to look into the fact as to who is catering to the need of the poor and who is not. Such comparative analysis may help us in understanding the social views of the new franchising model.

4) Accessibility, usability and affordability for the clients: Social enterprises are likely to ensure that their product or service is accessible in terms of location, usable in terms of technology, as there is normally skill deficit among the poor and affordable in terms of prices. They are likely to offer high performance products but at a low price without compromising on quality. There is a need to look into this matter. A franchise model has the scope to meet the criteria of accessibility in terms of location, in case the franchisee owners intend to set up their franchisee units in villages where they themselves do live. It is imperative that the

price and quality factors are also taken care of in terms of satisfaction of the target people.

5) Scalability: Although the franchisee owners are mostly from the Shia Momin (Chilea) community, their target customers are not likely to be limited to their own community people. However, this needs to be investigated. Since economies of scale and scope, as Awasthi argues, decide the viability of the products/services offered, social enterprises are likely to upscale their offering quickly. But, economies of scale may not be favourable in terms of village infrastructure, whereas, in terms of scope, village level franchisees have reasons to prosper.

6) A charismatic and visionary leadership to make the organisation cause centric or issue based: Starting a social enterprise requires enormous courage since one knows that such business is not going to pay immediate and high financial dividends. In the present case, Nadeem Jafri, the franchiser, has taken the initiative to build a franchising business networks based on his community connections, but his leadership quality would determine the future of this model in the long run.

7) Strong, committed and value driven management teams: The promoters of such enterprises need to motivate his team to adopt the same philosophy and commitment that he himself has. This is not an easy task. However, members of the same religious group or community may be motivated in the same line as has been conceived by the head of the community/group. This requires further investigation.

Social Entrepreneurs: Faith in Markets and Contribution to Poverty Alleviation

Social entrepreneurs think of business and profits, but at the same time, they think of the deprived people too. In this regard, Awasthi (2010) makes important observations: "We have seen that irrespective of the region, sector or the issue addressed, social enterprises have made their mark by significantly contributing to poverty alleviation. We also saw that all the persons behind these enterprises, the social entrepreneurs, were committed and most of them had total faith in markets. They believed in profits rather than charity or philanthropy." It is to be examined whether Hearty Mart owner has made an impression by establishing franchising relationships with the village level franchisees. Also, people involved in this franchising business do not have any faith in charity or philanthropy. Now, if they continue to look after the interest of the poor, they will be able to blend the concept of social entrepreneurship with the model of supermarket franchising chains.

Do Islamic Ethics have anything to do with (Social) Entrepreneurship?

Creation of livelihoods is one of the fundamental aspects of Islamic economics. Being involved in entrepreneurial activities not only creates livelihood for the entrepreneur himself but also creates jobs for others; and thus entrepreneurship receives entrepreneurial support from Islam. Moreover, in general, being attached to livelihoods is profoundly endorsed by Islamic ideology. We would, now, briefly discuss certain pertinent issues that would help us to understand the matter in relation to the theme of this section. Islam, currently the world's second largest religion (Hill 2008), is described in the *Qur'an* as the submission to the will of Allah or God (Cullen and Parboteeah 2008). The origins of Islam can be traced back to the Prophet Muhammad who is seen as the 'final agent of God's revelation' (Ludwig 2001: 428). There are two primary sources for Islam's ethical system: *Qur'an* and *Hadith*.[6] The first and foremost resource is the *Qur'an*, which is believed to be the verbatim word of God as preached by the Prophet Muhammad. The revelation of *Qur'an* did not occur all at once; rather, it was revealed step-by-step following the events that happened in the society in which Muhammad lived.

6. A collection of traditions containing sayings of the prophet Muhammad which, with accounts of his daily practice (the Sunna), constitute the major source of guidance for Muslims apart from the *Qur'an*.

The second primary source of Islamic ethics[7] is the *Hadith*, which is the record of the words, approvals, and practices of the Prophet Muhammad.

Islamic Ethics, Livelihood and Entrepreneurship

All the economic functions in the Islamic economics have been regulated by the concept of livelihood (*al-Rizq*) as well as lawful (*halal*) and unlawful (*haram*) sources of earnings (Ab. Aziz 2011). The term '*al-Rizq*' is applied to connote livelihoods and means of further production, which has been intimated by the Prophet Muhammad and predetermined by Allah (Borhan and Ab. Aziz 2009). How is it predetermined? As it is often said, for any sect which is a part of Islam, engaging in entrepreneurship is almost akin to a religious activity. Since the franchisers of the Hearty Mart franchising organisation, i.e. Nadeem Jafri and his partners, and the village level franchisees do all belong to Islamic religion, we may assume that, in this regard, they have received at least some motivation from their religious ideology. Nadeem Jafri himself chose entrepreneurship over a professional career. Islamic *Tusawwar* (Islamic conceiving) that relates Islam to business, as apparent from the verses of the *Qur'an* and the *Hadith*, is far-reaching and comprehensive. In this regard, Abu Sa'id[8] refers to the Prophet Muhammad-Rasulullah (PBUH). who said: "An honest and sincere businessman will be placed with the Prophet's Siddiqin and Al-Syuhada" (Hadith Hasan) (Al Misri 2007: 28-29).[9] Thus, the *Hadith* places the highest recognition to businessmen. Hamid and Sa'ari (2011) elaborate that, to reach this level, it is prescribed to hinder the negative elements and be honest, truthful and sincere. Businessmen are in constant struggle against the lure and seduction of *satan* on each sale and trade (*Al-Qaradawi*,

---

7. Islamic ethics, defined as "good character," historically took shape gradually from the 7th century and was finally established by the 11th century. It was eventually shaped as a successful amalgamation of the Qur'anic teachings.

8. Abu Sa'id was a very respected and dominant person in Islam with deep knowledge of the *Prophet's* life and sayings.

9. Cited in Hamid and Sa'ari (2011).

2001: 43).[10] In fact, an imam during the era of tabi'in was once asked about his preference between an honest businessman and a pious devotee who spent his life in prayer. He chose the businessman because he was constantly engaged in struggle. Muhammad et al. (2008) elaborate on the much reiterated concept of business as a form of struggle. *Al'Quran* manifests this encouragement to Muslims towards business through summons like: "seek to use all resources available on earth and open up opportunities for the same cause." Sinful resources are specifically banned and the words '*tijarah*' standing for business and '*al-bay*' standing for trade are specifically mentioned in Quranic verses. Business and trade are considered a necessary duty or part of the activities of a human being. In fact, this gives us an insight into the psyche of Nadeem, the franchiser, and the Shia Momin (Chilea) entrepreneurs, and their motivation for entrepreneurship.

The Principles of Islamic Ethics in Building an Enterprise

The idea of ethics in an enterprise is generally discussed within the framework of customer rights and good management of business (Oukil 2013). Theoretically, there are many principles of ethics in Islam that are derived from the *Qur'an* and *Hadith* of the Prophet Muhammad. However, for the purpose of this study, the Islamic business ethics that only correlate with social enterprise are discussed.

The sense of brotherhood creates a bond or a sense of unity in which all work together as a team. The cooperative and collaborative work within the team and between teams creates powerful drivers for innovative societal change. Collaboration is (may be) necessary for entrepreneurs to derive innovative solutions that go beyond the traditional thinking; and, as we can understand, individuals are the key vehicles for such transformation and innovation (Austin and Reficco 2009). However, with respect to the present study, we believe that without a good teamwork, it is difficult to build a franchising system. Thus, it is imperative that in the Hearty Mart System, there

10. Ibid.

should be teamwork among the Shia Momin members i.e. all the franchisees, franchiser and partners.

In an Islamic system, compatibility is theoretically found as far as business and ethics are concerned. As already indicated above, Islam stresses the link between business and religion. As we come to know from Islamic literature, Islam attempts to project a perfect way of life. Thus, in this line of thinking, Islamic business literature often emphasises the issues pertaining to the concept of business ethics in Islamic perspective. As said, in Islam, there is no separation between entrepreneurial activities and practising of religion. Islam supports one's involvement in entrepreneurship in the line of its own ethics and guiding principles based on *Al-Quran* and *Al-Hadith* to guide entrepreneurship operation (Oukil 2013). As regards specific sect within Muslim community, the members of the Shia Momin community follows the teachings of Syed Pir Mujahid Hussain Jafri, whose teachings are themselves guided by the *Qur'an*.

As mentioned, the literature on Islamic ethics and entrepreneurship has been studied by us in this chapter. Specifically, we have noted Islamic principles and values in relation to the present study. Muslim entrepreneurs are composed of conscientious people with high levels of faith, who are particularly concerned about making profits that are strictly originated from what is permissible. A conscientious Muslim entrepreneur is defined as a person who acts everywhere and always according to Islamic principles and values (Oukil 2013). Conscientious Muslim entrepreneurs are those who are convinced that faith-based behaviour will safeguard them from any wrongdoing. The main essence of spiritual or religious entrepreneurship exists in the person who is not greedy and selfish, and who does not abuse or exploit others. Hannafey (2003) has divided physical and spiritual dimensions of Islamic entrepreneurship. In his study, he finds that Islamic entrepreneurs make a balance between materialised and spiritual goals of enterprise. He has also argued that Islamic entrepreneurship is quite distinct from western and other religious entrepreneurship. Here, we must distinguish between those who merely practice Islam as a religion and those who practice it as a way of life (from practical point of view).

There are some studies emphasising importance of Islamic principles and values in business. Scholars such as Imam al-Ghazzali have emphasised morality in commerce, earnings, and works, and indicated that transitions are important in any business. Scholars such as Imam al-Ghazzali have emphasised morality in commerce, earnings, and works, and indicated that transitions are important in any business. Specifically according to al-Ghazali (2006) "the aim of business exchange and involvement is to create value to society and serving one's interests, while serving the community." As Muhammad et al. (2008) argue, according to the Islamic business worldview, an entrepreneur should have some important value-driven traits such as accountability, transparency, trustworthiness and customer respect. Muslim entrepreneurs profoundly believe that they will be accountable for whatever they do. Islam teaches that an entrepreneur must disclose information such as policies, activities, and programmes for community services to his customers and stakeholders. In this respect, revelation of information relating to use of resources and protection of the environment is also taken into account as far as transparency is concerned (Haniffa 2002). By maximising social welfare and by avoiding unjustified and unlawful enrichment, the entrepreneurs have the chance to augment their deeds, and hence gain respect from others and even blessings from Allah. As far as entrepreneurship is concerned, Imam Ghazzali (2003) has strongly emphasised fair returns and, at the same time, warned against any excessive rate of revenue, as it happens in Western profit-driven capitalism (Mehmet 1997). Along with the above values, other important matters such as truthfulness, benevolence, sincerity, trust, and honesty make the bulk of Islamic ethics (Muhammad et al. 2008).

The Islamic ethics and value system create the true personality of a Muslim entrepreneur. An entrepreneur's personality from Islamic perspective influences his/her actions and his/her ways of reacting to problems. This involves the tendency, ambitions, intuition to do mental, emotional and physical preparation. The Islamic values upheld by a Muslim entrepreneur will allow him/her to possess a high level of '*taqwa*' (God consciousness) for Allah. Therefore, the characteristics which differentiate a Muslim entrepreneur from a non-Muslim entrepreneur are the personalities that are based on Islamic values in thinking, behaviour and emotion (Yaacob and Azmi 2012).

Let us now look at some of the key characteristics of a Muslim entrepreneur in practice.

Trust

Scholars and practitioners widely acknowledge the importance of trust in business. Trust makes cooperative endeavours happen. Trust is a key to positive interpersonal relationships in various settings because it is central to how we interact with others (McKnight and Chervany 1996). Trust is another fundamental ethical principle of Islam. The essence of trust is the sense of accountability which implies the sense of having to appear before Allah and to be accountable for one's actions (Manan and Abdullah 2012). Being a part of Islam, the Shia Momin Community, as it seems, follows the principle of trust which is further reflected in their strong franchising networks.

Justice

Justice means to treat people equally and is a prerequisite of fairness in business. Justice is the sum total, in a sense, of all recognised rights and duties, as it often consists of nothing more than a balanced implementation of rights and duties. The *Qur'an* is emphatic on the objectivity of justice, so much so that it defies any level of relativity and compromise in its basic conception (Oukil 2013). In the context of its application in social enterprise activity, the principle of justice applies both literally and figuratively. In terms of the relationship between social enterprise manager and its subordinates, the principles of justice implies that managers should exercise fair and equal treatment to all workers regardless of genders, races, physical differences, religion and political beliefs. Indeed, skills, experience and attitude will determine the potential qualities of the workers. Additionally, Islam totally rejects the practice of favouritism and cronyism that lead to injustice in hiring and promoting employees[11] and in other matters. In fact, employees should be chosen or promoted based on their academic qualification, level of experience, moral qualities as well as their technical competency (Shaharuddin 2005). Islam does not aim to create a society of martyr-like entrepreneurs, doing business for a purely benevolent reason. Islam just wants to control man's propensity for covetousness and his love for possessions, not more than that (Beekun 1997). In this regard, there is similarity between Islamic entrepreneurship and social entrepreneurship.

Sincerity

Islam attaches great importance to the sincerity of intentions and actions in every walk of life (Abeng 1997). The performance of duties requires that all individuals in social enterprise type organisations work with sincerity and fidelity. One clear benefit can be produced by instilling sincerity in business deals. The workers are able to contribute to the high rate of productivity by speeding up production. In addition, such ethical aspect also discourages manipulation or exploitation of others for personal reasons (Ahmad 1991, McClaren 2013).

Truthfulness

Truthfulness is a basic ethical value in Islam. Islam is, in a way, the other name of truth. Allah speaks truth, and commands all Muslims to be straightforward and truthful in their dealings and utterances. Islam strongly condemns falsehood and deceit in any form (Ahmad 1991). Enterprise managers have to be honest, truthful and clear-cut in all of their conducting a business. There is no scope for cheating, swearing too much, speaking lies and false advertising in an Islamic framework of business. Once he chooses to become a Muslim, he must submit his will to Allah. He joins the collective of the *Ummah*, and assumes his rightful position as Allah's trustee on

---

11. It is considered that skills, experience and attitude should determine the potential qualities of the workers.

earth. To a certain extent, truthfulness is the obligations of a true Muslims' faith in Allah or what we call as Iman (Ahmad 1991).

Benevolence

Showing benevolence to others means fineness, proficiency or magnanimity in dealing with others. Along with the concept of justice, the concept of benevolence is also frequently repeated in the *Qur'an* and the *Hadith* (Hasanuzzaman 2003).

Conclusion

Thus, the Islamic perspective concerning ethical aspects of business enterprise has been presented in view of the *Qur'an* and *Hadith*. The ethical aspects are made up of five axioms, namely, trust, justice, sincerity, truthfulness, and benevolence. At least some of these have some links with the components of social entrepreneurship. For example, as far as justice is concerned, an Islamic entrepreneur, just like a social entrepreneur, takes care of the poor customers by controlling his personal desire for extremely high return, i.e. by offering them products at very reasonable price. But, let us try to understand the fact that Hearty Mart is a growing organisation. The franchisers and the franchisees want to grow. In true sense, it may not comply with all the rules/axioms of social entrepreneurship and Islamic entrepreneurship, but, after collecting more information from them, we can try to assess whether they are very close to the concept of social entrepreneurship or slightly close to it.

4

Some Conceptual Issues of a Community-Oriented Franchising Model

Introduction

In this chapter, we present a review of literature from organisational perspectives and, in this connection, we discuss various issues such as information asymmetries, bounded rationalities, and incomplete contracts. Also, we discuss the problems of motivation and coordination in the context of a community-oriented franchising network. These concepts are introduced under the broad heading of the fundamental problems of economic organisation. At the same time, we would like to discuss in this chapter the concept of trust within an institutional framework. We emphasise that institutional trust can evolve as social capital and thus can help build a new model of franchising.

Community-based Franchising

This study is concerned with the members of the Shia Momin Community (or Chilea community), who are living in urban and rural areas of Gujarat. Within a setting of various socio-religious groups/communities, the minority community may sometimes find the existing cultural environment somewhat external and complex (Alagh 2014), which may, in turn, create the problem of motivation as far as new initiatives are concerned. Under such conditions of bounded rationality, there may be reflection of the problem of information asymmetry (we elaborate it later in this chapter). In the safe confines of their own community, the Shia Momin people feel that they have secure property rights and trust. In addition, they feel greater security under the umbrella of the influence of the reputation of the community head. This perhaps stems from the common institutional culture and identity. In the larger external environment, it may not be unusual that the members of the community find themselves facing informational asymmetry and thus accordingly facing a situation of bounded rationality. In this situation, the motivation problem, as mentioned above, needs to be explained. Similarly, some aspects from the point of view of organisational perspectives also need to be explained (Alagh 2014). An interesting aspect is: how a hybrid franchising model determines the organisational coordination solution through dealing with community relationship, securing property rights, and ensuring institutional trust and culture (Douma and Schreuder 2008, Milgrom and Roberts 1992). The process may envisage empowerment of a rural community through the provision of new facilities and opportunities. Thus, there is a need to look into the process of creation of such franchising model. A model, which is decentralised in rural areas, provides scope to the rural people to grow through the new institutional development. In this regard, various organisation-related concepts are explained in this chapter. Thus, we try to understand a complex social and organisational mechanism while studying this franchising model.

Community-based Organisation: An Initial Description of Concepts and Themes

Motivation

People must be 'motivated' to carry out their productive activity. But, sometimes, this may not be an easy process. There may be lack of information about the external environment, especially at the bottom of the hierarchy. However, in a community of good network whatever information is available, there may be almost complete sharing of information within that particular community and within the organisation. But since, as assumed, there is lack of information about external environment, the phenomenon may lead to motivation deficit caused by asymmetric information and related problem such as moral hazard. This is a situation which can be termed as bounded rationality. Because of bounded rationality, the stakeholders may face a mismatch in terms of information flow between the main stream community and other communities and this can lead to communication failure (full or partial). However, motivation is a function of several factors, including information. Let us now discuss them.

Coordination

If there are reasonably flexible contracts and freedom of individual units in an organisational structure, the role of periodical supervision (regular, but not strictly formal) by the franchiser may be important. At the same time, rigid hierarchical structure may not be present in a franchising model, the characteristics of which represent hybrid organisational model. In this context, it is important to consider the role of the central authority in a franchising model. It plays a pivotal role in the organisation, especially when the organisation follows informal contracts. In the present case, the central authority may be Hearty Mart Super Market at Juhapura (or, for some reasons, Hearty Mart Enterprise [HME]), but, as we have seen in Chapter 2, both Hearty Mart Super Market at Juhapura and HME have flexible relations with the franchisees in terms of contractual relationship. By and large, the franchisees are independent and have a contract with the central authority of the Hearty Mart Franchising model. This might have had some impacts on the motivation of the franchisees. We will investigate this later.

Property Rights and Transaction Costs

The rights of individuals to exploit their resources for the use value are referred to as property rights (Eggertsson 1990). Enforcing property rights is "a method of assigning to particular individuals the 'authority' to select, for specific goods, any use from an unprohibited class of uses" (Alchian 1965: 130). The concept of property rights in new institutional economics goes beyond the legal concept of property rights and includes social norms (Eggertsson 1990) which are relevant while studying the Hearty Mart Franchising model. Another concept is transaction cost. Eggertsson (1990: 14) defines transaction costs as the costs that arise when individuals exchange ownership rights to economic assets. Matthews (1986: 906) defines transaction costs as the costs of arranging a contract ex-ante and monitoring and enforcing it ex-post, as opposed to production costs, which are costs of executing a contract. If transaction costs are high in an economy due to different non-economic reasons (social, cultural, political, etc.), then the economy may, in fact, suffer from economic decline due to such reasons. If non-economic processes affect economic activity, this may sometimes be attributed to organisation failure (e.g. failures of social organisations or communities) which may induce transaction costs due to which national wealth is not maximised (Eggertsson 1990). Strong cultural networks of any community can be an alternative way out and can motivate the agents to carry out economic activities. We have to look into this matter later.

Information Flow through Organisation

There is an issue that relates to a question whether there is use of both prices and alternative organisation mechanisms operational in this franchising model. That is: is it a mechanism where prices are playing a central role; or do mutual communication, norms, reputation, sharing and other related facets play a role in the franchiser-franchisee relation at Hearty Mart. Having built up the context, we introduce the concept of information. Douma and Schreuder (2008: 14-15) argue that the coordination mechanism(s) in any situation will depend mainly on the information requirements inherent in it with the price mechanism many a time complemented or substituted by organisational coordination mechanisms. Price may not absorb all the information necessary to enable the execution of transactions. Thus, fundamental information problems, though possibly not resolved by the price system, can, however, be dealt by means of organisational coordination. Organisations thus arise as solutions to information problems. They are more suited to deal with certain information problems than are markets.

The market-organisation mix depends on the particular information requirements of a situation. Information and communication costs are, to a large extent, often seen to have determined the market-organisation mix and the relative efficiency of the two broad coordination mechanisms between markets and organisations.

Institutions

Organisations live in an environment that is shaped and created within the economic, social, political and other related milieu and such milieu provides ultimate selection mechanism for determining about which organisations can survive and be successful (Douma and Schreuder 2008: 16-17). The environment also creates and shapes all markets by exerting economic, social, political and other pressures. An institutional environment, based on the reputation of the sect-head of the Shia Momin community, may be effective in minimising the external pressure and thus introduce a model through cooperation and coordination.

New Institutional System

Economics has been related with scarcity of resources and maximising the output out of the scarcity (Robbins 1935). Hence, there has been a kind of obsession with the logic of choice. This, in Coase's (1960) view, has meant that there has been a divorce of the theory of economics from many relevant subject matters of economics which have far more diverse depth and ramifications than just the ones that are embedded in the logic of choice.

The need for a different approach to economic development emphasising the institutional aspects comes from different reactions of several mechanisms within the society and market. A search for an alternative institutional structure of the economic system, where property right is ensured through socio-cultural norms may be carried out as far as the Hearty Mart model is concerned. In this respect, the exigencies of its internal and external organisational environment may also be some of concerns. Influenced by Coase and Eggertson, as indicated above, theories that examine the role of institutional systems and structures do, to some extent, interest us and thus motivate us to delve into further details with respect to Hearty Mart model.

Franchising Model: Some Detailed Theoretical Underpinning

Let us now elaborate the relevant issues with a view to understanding the present case from broader theoretical contexts.

Coordination and Management

As we are dealing with an organisational model, we need to find out which decisions are to be centralised (at the franchiser level) and which ones are to be left to individual decision-makers (at the franchisee level). It is important to know how the centralised decisions are being made and, in that process, what information is obtained from outside the organisation to support these decisions? Also, how the centralised choices that delimit the decentralised decisions are to be communicated to the individual decision makers? Usually, solving this problem in firms is the task of senior management, as is the solution of the design problem of setting and communicating strategy (Milgrom and Roberts 1992: 118). Now, the issue of coordination comes in.

A higher need for coordination improves horizontal communication but worsens vertical communication (Alonso et al. 2008). How an organisation deals with both centralisation and flexibility (or, maintaining a balance between these two) with regard to their functioning is an interesting matter. In this respect, delegation of authority and responsibility across the franchisees is an important aspect. An illustration of this may possibly relate to the delegation of the responsibility of purchasing decision, pricing decision and other matters relating to the day-to-day running of franchising stores.

Some Organisational Aspects

As regards the role of hierarchy and supervision in a community-oriented franchising firm, there may not be any authoritarian control; the arrangement may simply be a contractual structure, subject to continuous renegotiations with the central agent. The contractual structure enhances efficient organisation of team production (Alchian and Demetsz 1972: 794). In some cases, the popular definition of rigidity of authority and supervision in a hierarchical structure in a firm may be hugely off the mark. As in the case of Hearty Mart, there is a non-judicial contract between the franchiser and the franchisee, with flexibility inherent in it. In such case, there may not be any sort of compulsion or force or dominance by the central authority over the franchisees. The firm represents an alternative to organising production that is based on market transactions. In such firms, non-hierarchical, alternative, administrative decision-making process makes things simple. Actually, the solution of the firm would be adopted whenever the administrative costs of the firm were less than the costs of the market transactions. For an efficient administrative decision-making process, coordination plays an instrumental role (Coase 1960: 16-17).

The first task relevant for solving the coordination problem is to maintain a balance between the choices of centralisation and decentralisation. Second is to pursue and guide the decentralised decision-making process. The final task is to set strategies and communicate the decentralised decisions, and the limitations that arise therein, to all the stakeholders.

Hybrid Form of Organisation

There are many governance structures which fall between ideal markets and ideal organisations (Douma and Schreuder 2008: 338-39). Let us take franchising as an example. Under franchising models, some franchisees are owned and operated by the parent company, while the rest are owned and operated by local entrepreneurs. The parent company goes for a contract with the local entrepreneurs, giving them the right to operate under its name. Such a contract is called a franchise contract. In such a contract, the two parties that take part are the franchiser (the parent company) and the franchisee (the local entrepreneur owning and operating a unit).

The franchiser usually develops a formula for operating the units. That formula consists of a range of products (including the way those products have to be prepared), a house style (which refers to things such as the furnishing of the unit, the uniform of personnel and how customers should be treated) and a brand name. Under the franchise contract, the franchisees are allowed to use that formula in return for a fee (usually a fixed amount, plus a percentage of sales).

If we first define a hybrid form loosely as a form of governance somewhere between market and organisation, then franchising fits that definition. Coordination between franchiser and franchisee does not take place through the market mechanism only. In fact, other coordination mechanisms play an important role: standardisation of work processes (for food production), standardisation of norms (for the house style) and direct supervision (the franchiser monitors the behaviour of the franchisee in order to protect the value of the brand name), among others. Hybrid form of an organisation can be more precisely defined as a set of organisations such that transaction between those organisations takes place simultaneously by means of the market mechanism and various other coordination mechanisms (Douma and Schreuder 2008). The Hearty Mart Franchising Model is a typical example of such a Hybrid Organisational Model.

New Franchising Model: Contracts, Information and Incentives

In general, business models follow the narrow and static understanding of contracts with hard and precise terms. There is a need to investigate whether flexibility could be (or has been) incorporated into contracting processes (Nystén-Haarala et al. 2010). If flexibility is found, then identifying the factors behind it can lead us to gain further insights.

Bounded Rationality

As sometimes seen, formulating and enforcing a complete and perfect contract in actual transaction are fraught with problems. In a situation where external cultural condition is complicated and easy information flow is sometimes interrupted, contingencies inevitably arise, which have not been planned for and, when they do, the parties must find ways to adapt (Milgrom and Roberts 1992: 127-29). These adaptations are possible when there are flexibilities.

In general terms, problems of imperfect commitment may crop up in the case of incomplete and unenforceable contracts. Even if a contingency can be foreseen and planned for and contractual commitments can be enforced, before the contract is signed, one of the bargainers may have relevant private information which may interfere in the possibility of reaching a value-maximising agreement. This opens the possibility of self-interested misbehaviour, and the recognition of this moral hazard problem limits the contracts that can be written and enforced (Milgrom and Roberts 1992: 127-29).

Consequently, the party's individual interests under actual contracts will not necessarily be properly aligned, and this leaves room for behaviour with self-interest to thwart the realisation of efficient plans. The motivation problem then relates to overcoming these difficulties to the extent possible. This involves realising the fact that individual's self-interested behaviour can constrain a task that can actually be accomplished. Then it is necessary to design efficient plans and systems that would attempt to overcome these constraints. Doing so requires a detailed understanding of the various causes of imperfect contracting, of the consequences of the various sorts of contracting difficulties, and of the responses that have emerged.

The inability of certain franchisees to follow the dictum of detailed attention to their franchiser and patient handling of their business with limited margins in the first few years leading to stores closing down is an illustration of such a constraint mentioned above.

Contractual Responses to Bounded Rationality

When contracts are incomplete, the aligning can be imperfect. This implies a situation of information asymmetry (Douma and Schreuder 2008: 338-9). Hart and Holmstrom (1986) have a valuable discussion of incomplete contracting. Information asymmetry is a situation where information is available but it is unevenly distributed. The problem of hidden information is an ex-ante information problem (Arrow 1985: 3). It is possible for one to have complete information about his/her own community business but he/she may have limited information about external environment. This lack of information about outside environment possibly does not exist as far as the entrepreneur, i.e. Nadeem himself in the present case, is concerned, but it exists the lower levels of the franchising networks.

However, in some case, post-contractual opportunism may arise because actions that have efficiency consequences are not freely observable and this may satisfy one's private interest at other's expense, and the phenomenon is known as moral hazard. Moral hazard is an exposit problem of hidden action; it refers to actions that parties in a transaction may take after they have agreed to execute the transaction (Pauly 1968). A franchisee dealing with independent wholesalers on his own without informing the Hearty Mart central authority is an example.

The above moral hazard problem arises when agent and principal have differing individual objectives and the principal cannot easily determine whether the agent's reports and actions are being taken in pursuit of the principal's goals or are self-interested misbehaviour (Ross 1973). Jensen (1983) differentiates between principal-agent relationship and positive agency theory, the former focusing on preferences, information and uncertainty for the parties to the contract in the principal-agent relationship and the latter more on external environment, information and monitoring of the contract and less on the actual factors affecting the principal-agent relationship.

The general business problem in which each party that enters into a contract gets worried about being forced in the future to accept disadvantageous terms, e.g. after it has sunk an investment, is called the hold-up problem. This may be reflected through a possible mismatch between strategies of Hearty Mart Franchiser(s) and activities of Hearty Mart franchisees, in which the latter may not follow the first due to lack of trust. However, this proposition needs to be verified through fieldwork. Klein et al. (1978) were the first scholars to emphasise and elaborate the great importance of the hold-up problem for the analysis of business institutions and practices. The hold-up problem is a special case of Coase's (1960) transaction cost analysis which focuses on the possible transaction with individuals rather than on integrated firm. Once we attempt to add empirical detail to Coase's fundamental insight that a systematic study of transaction costs is necessary to explain particular forms of economic organisation, we find that many long-term contractual relationships (such as franchising) blur the line between market and the firm. "It may be more useful to merely examine the economic rationale for different types of particular contractual relationships in particular situations and consider the firm as a particular set of inter related contracts" (Klein et al. 1978: 326).

Contracts, Ownership and Property Rights

Contracts legitimise the authority to transact in business with the help of the property rights over the assets of ownership.

Property Rights and Transaction Costs

Coase (1960) provided the initial modern contribution to economic analysis of property rights, emphasising that the ability of parties to trade and contract lies at the centre of the theory. Alchian and Kessel's (1962) insight was that the set of rules (regarding the distribution of property rights) determined the level of output of the firm because they determined the incentives of each individual. Property rights are therefore defined as the ability to freely exercise a choice over a good/a service.

It is common to distinguish three categories of property rights: First, there are the rights relating to use of asset; second, there is the right to earn income from an asset and contract over the terms with other individuals, if any. Third, there is the right to transfer permanently to another party ownership rights over an asset—i.e. to sell an asset (Eggertsson 1990: 35). The property right literature, as discussed in the article by Alchian and Kessel (1962), argues that there is a monotonic relationship between property rights and wealth. Other things equal, individuals prefer better defined property rights over poorer defined ones because they prefer more wealth to less.

When the state imposes some limits on exclusive rights, it is customary to refer to these restrictions as the attenuation of property rights. This concept of attenuation of property rights is absent in the basic neoclassical model. However, in the real world we find that property rights are either not properly delineated or are otherwise attenuated because of state restrictions (in case state restriction is there). "If transaction costs are prohibitively high then property rights will neither be established nor maintained and property rights will be zero" (Allen 2000). If there is lack of clarity in contracts regarding the ownership of the assets then there will be inefficiency in the working. Similarly, if there are high inefficiency costs then ownership rights over asset will be restricted. Against this theoretical construct, we need to study the nature of the contract in Hearty Mart franchising system.

Issues Related to Information

As said above, Hearty Mart uses hybrid organisational mechanism to coordinate among various units. Information is exchanged through its own channels across the organisational structures. For efficient choices, it is necessary to have information about individual tastes, technological opportunities and resource availabilities as far as the franchisees are concerned (Douma and Schreuder 2008). Once this information at the level of the franchisees—which are dispersed across districts and somewhat localised in nature—is available, processing and sharing can be done at the headquarter level, i.e. at the franchiser level. Solving this problem requires a mix of decentralised system of information collection at the individual franchisee level in the villages and centralised information and knowledge transmission by the Ahmedabad-based franchiser.

Information may be needed for additional purposes as well. For example, different types of information may be useful for the generation of innovative ideas. Sometimes ingenuity and resources would be required to achieve the social development of the community members involved, apart from the natural working of the franchising system in Hearty Mart.

Let us have a look at information creation in retail markets—for instance, Hearty Mart. How does an individual retail-franchisee draw attention of the people to the quality of the products in his shop? One may be curious about why the various products are displayed so differently. We submit that a major reason for these differences is the variation in quality that may be expected from different brands.

Then again, there are limitations to what can be achieved in terms of information generation by product display. For many retail products, an intermediate solution is to standardise quality as much as possible. Through media advertisements and other means, we learn to identify certain brand names as signals of particular quality classes. Also, we see common brand names for different products (e.g. soups and sauces).

The above discussions convey that the quality of product is important information, which the producers and retailers want to communicate to the consumer in some useful ways. Suppose, as indicated above, that the quality of the product is not yet known (to anyone), it may be possible to signal the quality of the products available in a retail store through an organisational means with regard to the goods. This often involves a rapport between the retailer and his customers through which subtle communication on a daily basis is achieved. Thus, considering the local issues/factors, there is a need to allow franchisees leeway and space to direct and determine communication in the shop in the ways they want.

In case of Hearty Mart, there is the obvious case where there is the possibility that the franchiser (Hearty Mart) may have more information about the product than the franchisees and so the greater risk is located with the franchiser.

Institutional Trust as Social Capital

Handling functional aspects in the organisation, on the one hand, and dealing with social expectations of the public concerned, on the other, build the (informal) framework of a company which provides 'return in cooperation' and produce reputation capital including providing long-term competitive advantages. The higher the reputation capital, the less the costs for supervising and exercising control (Klewes and Wreschniok 2010). As explained by Douma and Schreuder (2008), "in the absence of the essential institutional safeguards, impersonal exchange does not exist, except in cases where strong ethnic or religious ties make reputation a viable underpinning".

Promises, beliefs, trust and loyalty—all are also factors which can avoid moral hazard when business transactions happen in a community. At the same time, the incidence of moral hazard may be present in a very low scale among people whose personal interactions are intense and who can predict almost accurately the others behaviour. Mutual trust nurtured through close personal relations works as an effective brake on community moral hazards (Hayami 1997: 241). Close business ties and cooperative commercial relationship lead to, to some extent, avoidance of factors such as private business risks and uncertainties. One way to achieve this relationship (trust) is to shift from spot transactions between anonymous agents mostly based on the price parameter to long term continuous transactions (Hayami 1997: 245, Geertz 1978). In this context, personal interaction is important. Mutual trust created by long-term continuous transactions can be further reinforced by multiple intensified transactions (Hayami 1997: 245, Bardhan 1980, Bell 1988, Hayami and Otsuka 1993 and Besley 1995).

Betrayal may become difficult in relationships of mutual trust created through long term and multiple transactions. Such relationships would not only be effective in curbing moral hazards between the parties that have come into contract but would also support collaborative initiatives within the wider community. People who were benefiting from interactions based on trust would not want to trade with one who was known to have betrayed his business partner before, in terms of both moral sentiment and risk calculation (Hayami 1997: 245). Further analysis in this context considering trust as social capital can be found in the writings of the authors such as Arrow (1974), Dasgupta (1988), Putnam (1993) and Seabright (1993). In the Shia Momin Chilea Community, trust may be seen to be natural result of the reputation of the family of community head (i.e. family of Nadeem) and the concomitant culture of the community itself.

Complimentarity between Strategies and Activities

The degree of profit achieved in such a model may depend on the complementary fit between the central enterprise and franchisees in terms of strategies planned and the resulting activities. This degree of complementarity is what lies behind the success of the model (Burlow et al. 1985). Thus, a feasible proposition is as follows: If the franchisees follow through the strategies planned out by the central authority in the model with patience and sagacity, their business might grow. As far as this proposition is concerned, there is a need to delve into the matter with regard to the case of Hearty Mart.

Conclusion

The above review explains the economic logic of low margins operated in a franchising model using small rural Chilea community entrepreneurs as franchisees related with the organisational logic which is underlined by the limits of the market as well as limits of conventional organisational forms. Further is underlined the logic of the framework of organisational hybrids such as franchising networks expressed in terms of the problem of coordination, motivation, information, property rights and institutions. The fit between strategy of Hearty Mart franchising model and the resulting processes in the model, leading to complementarities which are sought to achieve a good fit resulting in satisfying community goals and yet leading to profit. A detailed study of the literature on these aspects is presented which when combined with the facts of the case leads to a delineation of an alternative organisational structure for the model.

5

Analysis of the Hearty Mart Model from the Perspectives of Social Entrepreneurship

Introduction

In this chapter, we are going to examine the Hearty Mart franchisee model on the basis of various pillars of social entrepreneurship. As we know, social entrepreneurship is primarily about the passion which drives certain individuals—passion to 'change' the world, passion to improve the way things are happening around (Awasthi 2010). We would like to study whether there is a reflection of such passion in the Hearty Mart Model. Through Hearty Mart, the franchiser Nadeem wanted to introduce some 'changes' within his community. Although Nadeem's own supermarket store is located in city area, he has developed networks and business contracts with his franchisees that are located in villages and small rural towns (rural growth centres) in Gujarat. Supermarkets of modern format in so called traditional/rural areas offer rural people an opportunity to practice modern shopping. Usually, large-scale franchisers (e.g. Future Group) would want to make contract with the franchisees that are located in already developed place, keeping in view the economies of scale of the location. Conversely, villages and rural growth centres are endowed with poor or underdeveloped infrastructure. Moreover, per-capita income of the population in rural areas may be found to be much lower than that of their city counterparts. Naturally, villages and small rural towns are not the destinations of the large-scale organised retailers. On the other hand, it may not be always true that the village people would want to avoid modern grocery shops only due to their traditional mindset; rather, they may want to welcome opening up of such shops in their locality if such shops operate within the reach of affordability of the local people. Although the Hearty Mart initiative is driven by a particular community networks, the idea of entering into contracts with the village level franchisees deserves credit as a pioneering initiative and passion for change. The initiative is also likely to help the community to shift their mind from a ghettoised territory to a larger world through different types of commercial exchanges. However, let us now study the Hearty Mart case in the light of the conceptual model as formulated by Dinesh Awasthi (2010). The model is summarised in Figure 5.1.

Figure 5.1

Conceptualisation of Hearty Mart as a Social Enterprise

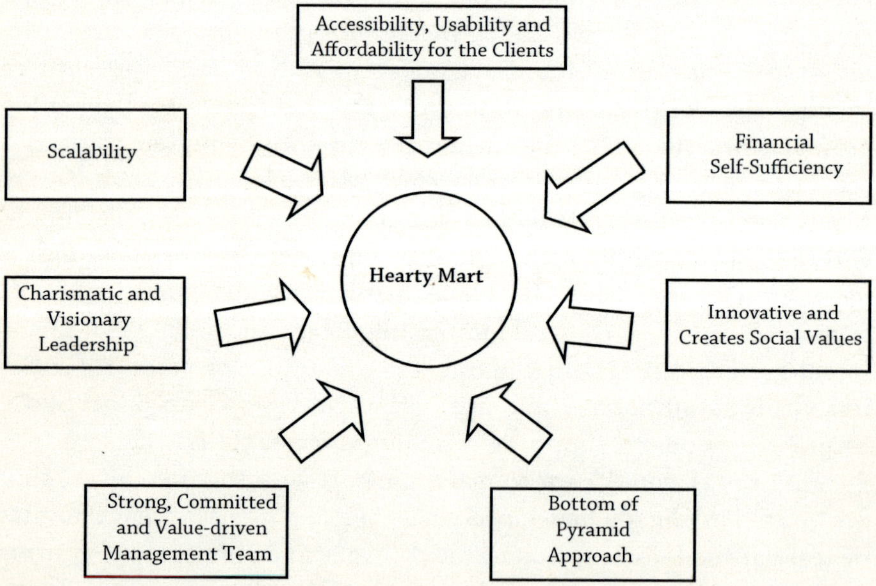

Source: Adapted from Awasthi (2010).

Bottom of Pyramid

As often said, the social entrepreneurs use market-based model but do not bypass the poor. Instead, they treat poor as valuable customers and consumers. The importance of this approach comes from the experience which often shows that economic growth has been uneven and has bypassed the poor. In a similar vein, it is also argued that fast growth has taken place mostly in the urban pockets, leaving the rural areas in waiting for the slow trickle-down benefit. Let us not say that the Hearty Mart model has so far been successful in bringing a 'huge' social change; but, at least, the organisation has decided to operate within the poor as well as in backward areas, using the market-based model. Moreover, after Nadeem started his own supermarket store in Ahmedabad and subsequently floated his ideas of developing new franchisees, some of his community members (i.e. members from the Shia-Chilea community) responded back spontaneously and positively. Several of his religious followers wanted to join his hands as franchisees. In some way, this can be viewed as 'peoples' participation' in an initiative that wants to reach-out to the places beyond the core urban commercial boundary. Overall, the Hearty Mart project has been able to raise the level of well-being of some people in Chilea community. For example, as said earlier, Hearty Mart Enterprise (HME) has employed a number of poor people from Santhal village. And, regular bus service is provided to them for their travel (both home to work and work to home) at free of cost. In a similar vein, the Vadgam franchisee told that he has picked up the employees for his supermarket store mostly from the pool of unemployed youth from the poor families of the locality. Some of them did not have secured or regular jobs. Rather, they were engaged in very low paid jobs and their life was at the mercy of daily wage payers. One day they may get work and the very next day employment may not be available. Several of the Hearty Mart employees who come from village told us that earlier they had gone through partial starvation but now their life has changed.

Asad Khan Pathan, the Vadgam franchisee, reported that he is now very happy since the people who are working in his supermarket store do not go to sleep hungry anymore. However, he categorically told that while profit is an important aspect of his venture, his foremost goal is to give customers optimum satisfaction and his next goal is to look after his employees' interest. Similarly, Surat franchisee is also found to be employing the poor youth from his community (i.e. Shia Chilea community). The example of generosity at Hearty Mart does not end here. In fact, other franchisees such as Sadiq Ali of Dholka are in the list, who wanted to be employment generators for the people of their locality and they have achieved considerable success in their endeavours.

Let us give a different example. The franchisee at Kanai had been running a grocery shop for a long time with a very low level of return before he joined Hearty Mart as a franchisee. With Nadeem's help, his grocery shop was converted into a very different set-up. A shift was experienced in the quality of goods in the shop. Hearty Mart management helped them by sharing complete information about interiors and procurement procedure to convert a traditional grocery shop to a modern general store. Consequently, his customer base went up. Thus, his union with Hearty Mart helped him to raise his income from a very low level to a reasonably good level.

As far as social entrepreneurship is concerned, both—growth of a business on the one hand, and catering to the needs of the poor customers on the other—are important. If growth of the business does not take place, it would be difficult to serve the poor. Wajir Ali, one of the partners of Nadeem Jafri, explained it very well. He told that they have a dual price policy for customers in Hearty Mart. For the products of daily consumption, they aim for very nominal profits, whereas they do not follow the same policy for the lifestyle products. This indicates that they want to follow the rules of the market while, at the same time, they do not want to ignore the issues of the needy people. In this regard, the Surat franchisee has told us that his policy is to reach-out to lower and middle income group people. He gave two clear-cut examples. One, whenever he receives discounts from the wholesalers and dealers, he passes on good enough of it to the customers. Two, he is selling many products such as hair oil, tooth paste, shampoo, snacks items, some spices, foodgrains, among others, at below MRP prices. Not only this, some of the franchisees such as one at Kanai offers discounts at festive seasons so that the LIG (low income group) is accommodated and can enjoy the festival at ease.

Is there any other model that is similar to Hearty Mart retail chains? Not really. But, Aravind Eye Care System, Tamil Nadu, has set some example of addressing the need of people living at bottom of pyramid of the society through their 'chain of hospitals.' Their treatment is not free for all. They charge fees for the non-poor while they provide free treatment to the poor. Over the period, they have expanded as a 'chain of hospitals' consisting of centre for manufacturing synthetic lenses, institute for training, institute for research, etc. Another example is Self Employed Women's Association (SEWA) in Gujarat which is an organisation of poor, self-employed women workers. These are women who earn a living through their own labour or small businesses. They have a marketing channel through their cooperatives.

Innovative and Creates Social Value

As the Hearty Mart franchiser told, prior to Hearty Mart was established in Jethipura, the people in the concerned village had no access to a large set of branded products. Hearty Mart has opened up an opportunity through its village level outlets by introducing branded items to the villagers. Villages have been exposed to all brands available in the FMCG (fast moving consumer goods) basket. As said in Chapter 2, Hearty Mart sells some products in its own brand names. For example, spices are sold in the brand name of 'Chef ki pasand' for hotel supplies. Spices are supplied to the franchisee outlets under the brand name of 'Good Time.' For tea, the company owns two brands 'Day Break' and 'Adarsh,' and, for quality rice, it owns the brand name of 'Hearty Mart Premium Basmati'. Since, for these products, quality is maintained by the franchiser itself and thereby sold to the village level customers under its own brands, this approach creates a social value among the villagers. Moreover, they purchase branded items at relatively low prices.

In order to reduce the cost of the products and to sell them to the customers at lower price, several franchisees, as they said, procure some items from the local poor producers. For example, Dholka franchisee told us that they purchase puffed rice, papad, pickles etc. from local small producers. He told that if he wanted to buy these products from Ahmedabad, it would have cost him more than what it costs now. Thus, local procurement has helped him to reduce the cost of these products and thus offer some benefits to the poor customers. Hence, this gives him extra opportunity in marketing such products. Meta franchisee told that they procure tea from local processor. The local processor uses a brand name called 'Green Bungalow' for his product. Thus, through this, two purposes are served. One, a local as well as relatively unknown brand is being promoted; two, the franchisee is in a position to offer quality good to the customers at relatively low price. Being influenced by this strategy, this franchisee is now planning to expand village level purchases to a much greater scale in the coming days. Similarly, Surat and Kanai franchisees also told that they are currently procurring some products from the local producers and they are thinking of expanding this in the future. Nadeem is nurturing pro-poor as well as innovative ideas, and his franchisees are no different from him.[1]

If village level supermarket is considered to be an 'innovative venture,' such new idea might have needed some aggressive penetration strategies. But, Nadeem, the franchiser, has always been insisting his partners and franchisees on pursuing social values that are connected to Islamic value system or Islamic ethics. In this regard, Wajir Ali (one of the partners of Nadeem) told that he had a misconception as he thought that religion and business cannot go hand in hand, because principles of these two streams are very different. After he met Nadeem, he understood that religion has something to do with business, especially some aspects of religion can be very well implemented in business. Religion teaches one not to cheat a customer in quantity; not to over praise the product for increasing sale; not to forget promises that were made to the customers; and so on. Realising his social responsibility towards his community, he has future plans to bear the school fees of the kids of his employees as a CSR (corporate social responsibility).

1. For example, sometimes poor villagers are found to possess crumbled notes and they do not know about what to do with that. Asad Khan Pathan, the Vadgam franchisee, has put a notice at the entrance of his store, showing that they do accept crumbled notes. This way he attracts customers who have crumbled notes. Poor villagers can purchase items in exchange of their crumbled notes and, later, Asad Khan Pathan exchanges the notes with the bank.

The Jethipura Hearty Mart supermarket store is found to be a unique and innovative initiative. This franchisee is not constituted by one or a few persons; rather it has manifested as a cooperative group where many villagers have participated as direct stakeholders. Perhaps, the villagers have taken such initiative owing to the fact that earlier there has been no retail outlet in their village. We describe this in further detail later in this chapter.

Financial Self-Sufficiency

Nadeem Jafri told that the purpose of establishing Hearty Mart is not to run the franchising business based on the philosophy of the charities. It is a profit making initiative. The people who are involved in this venture—either as franchiser, or as franchisee—do not consider that they are involved in any type of philanthropy. However, within the operational domain of Hearty Mart, some characteristics or aspects of social entrepreneurship are evident. As already indicated above, all the franchisees told that they offer some discount on most of the products to the customers. We would discuss this soon, but one thing is evident that they want to reachout to all kinds of households—i.e. rich, middle-class and poor. If they want to target the rich only, then it will be considered an organisation with niché customer base. But they do not want to target the rich only. Targeting the poor has also helped their business to grow. The franchisees located in Meta and Surat have categorically told that cutting in prices led to increase in sale and thus this has finally led to increase in profit. So, the strategy that they adopted includes lowering the price of the products, on the one hand, and to attract greater number of village people as well as maintain profit earning, on the other hand. As mentioned above, all the franchisees are in no philanthropy business, and indeed they are businessmen but with social responsibility. For an instance, Asad Khan Pathan has taken the distributorship of certain products, from some companies so that he can give that extra leverage to his customers over and above the routine discounts which other small grocery shops cannot even think of. Meta franchisee told us that he sells goods at highly discounted rates during religious seasons (a social cause). Kanai franchisee stock up goods in advance particularly when they are available at the cheaper rates and passes the benefits received to the customers. Though the prices are competitive at Hearty Mart, none of them compromises with the quality of the product, even when it is produced by local producer. Quality is assured at Hearty Mart.

Accessibility, Usability and Affordability for the Customer

As Awasthi (2010) said, social enterprises are likely to ensure that their product or service is accessible in terms of location, useable in terms of technology as there is normally skill deficit among the poor, and affordable in terms of prices. All the Hearty Mart franchisees are located in the villages and this has made possible for the villagers to access a supermarket system/format in their own locality. Let us cite the case of Jethipura. Earlier, there had not been a single retail shop in Jethipura village of Sabarkantha district. People of Jethipura used to go to Jadar market which is 5 km away from their place. In all respects, this was really very inconvenient for the residents of Jethipura. Even for a minor item, they had to go to Jadar market. After the Hearty Mart outlet came into being, it was a big relief for the villagers. Now, even the women and children can go to the Hearty Mart general store and purchase the required items. They can repeatedly visit the general store and purchase an available item in small quantity according to their needs.

We have observed that all the franchisees use electronic billing system which the other shops in the same areas do not use. Moreover, since they have installed computerised inventory management systems, the franchisees are regularly updated about their sales and stocks and customers do thereby always find the products available that they want to buy from the Hearty Mart outlets. Besides, the customers can directly pick up the products from the racks that are displayed in the store for sale. Like other big supermarkets, Hearty Mart does not provide any trolley facility but the customers are given the choice of using baskets instead.

Most of the ordinary village shops do not provide plastic bags to the customers to carry the purchased items while they are getting out of the shop. Hearty Mart franchisees provide each customer with certain plastic bag for carrying their goods. Most of the Hearty Mart franchisees provide home delivery service to the customers who opt for the same. Usually, home delivery service is not available in villages. In this regard, Hearty Mart has introduced a unique service for its customers. As of now, the home delivery service is available in Juhapura, Vadgam, Ilol, Meta, Dholka, and Chaapi. The Hearty Mart saral shops in Kanai, Pipodar and Jethipura have anyway very small set-up as the villages they serve are small.

Moreover, the village customers have got an access to many modern products such as 'branded' staple food, cornflakes, liquid washing detergent, different types of fruit juices and *sharbat*, branded pickles, packaged ghee, instant cook snacks (e.g. maggi, pasta etc.), liquid chocolate, after-shave gel and deodorant, among others. In this regard, one issue needs to be discussed. Hearty Mart has a very important integration strategy. Some big and branded companies like HUL and P&G do not give discounts to small entrepreneurs. As described in chapter 2, Nadeem has set up an intermediary company called HME which acts like a distributor. On behalf of all the franchisees, it raises collective demand which induces its bargaining power with the giant companies. This way it earns some discounts on bulk purchase. And these benefits are later passed to the customers in the form of low price.

The Dholka franchisee has given a good example of how he accommodates the poor customers through his policies. If two toothpastes together are offered at discounted price by the manufacturer, the price may be affordable to the middle and high income groups but may not be affordable to the LIG because purchase of two toothpastes at a time would require greater cash even at discounted price. Since the purchasing power of LIG is limited and some of them are in daily wage-based employment, they may want to buy single toothpaste at discounted price because of non-availability of sufficient cash at their disposal. Due to limited cash in their hands, they may prefer to buy single piece rather than a pack of two pieces even if the latter is more beneficial than the former. The well-to-do customer may afford bulk purchase at a time, whereas the poor may want to visit the retailers for small purchase and when cash is available to them. Hence, the Dholka franchisee has adopted suitable discount policies in favour of all types of customers. He keeps introducing new and innovative ideas of discount, which are affordable to the LIG.

During festival seasons, financial pressure on poor people gets high, because they want to fulfil their festive desires while their financial capacity is quite limited. At such times, special prices of different products give the poor customers much respite. Most of the Hearty Mart retail outlets offer special prices for different products so that they become affordable to the poor. For example, the Kanai franchisee reported that it offers special discounts on various products for the customers during festive seasons. The Meta franchisee told that they sell various goods at subsidised rates during religious functions. The Dholka franchisee has also confirmed this. He gives discounts on the products which has highest demand in the festive seasons (for example, sugar during Diwali, dates during Ramzan, etc.).

Scalability

People of Chilea community are located in different pockets of Gujarat. Currently, Hearty Mart has nine franchisees that are operating in different districts of Gujarat. According to Nadeem, there are opportunities to open more number of franchisees in the state. Prospective franchisees are in touch with Nadeem and some of them are in the pipeline to open franchisees in the near future. Nadeem would not like to confine his franchisee business within the Chilea community business networks only. He has a desire to move beyond his community boundary. For example, he categorically told that if non-Chileas are interested in opening Hearty Mart franchisees, he would extend his cooperation towards them. As an evidence, currently they have one non-Chilea as a franchisee in the team, and they are looking for others who are enough competent to take the responsibility of social enterprise. Thus, the current trend of his increasingly growing franchising networks indicates that there is prospect to upscale his offering through the new franchisees in the future. But Nadeem is little reluctant in moving very fast. He told us that with every bit of success he wants to stop, enjoy and then forge ahead to achieve new heights. He is the man who believes that one should think before leap. Hence, though he is getting ample opportunity to grow his business, he does not want to just spread without thorough and deep insight into it. He also gave us an example that one of the MNCs wanted to invest in his venture. They approached him but he refused to join the hands for two basic reasons. The very first reason is that an MNC will not be willing to give franchisees to the uneducated villagers residing in rural areas. They would rather prefer a developed market as their main motto will be to earn highest possible profits. The social responsibility which Nadeem has been carrying out will not be of utter importance to them. Secondly, if they give franchise to a person just by analysing the capacity of the market of the prospective franchisee's area, they may fail to get substantial result which in turn might fail and it may adversely affect brand Hearty Mart.

Several franchisees such as Vadgam Hearty Mart, Dholka Hearty Mart, and Meta Hearty Mart told that they would like to expand their supermarket stores. Vadgam Hearty Mart has categorically said that they are growing fast and to cope up with the growth, they are going to shift to a nearby three-storied building where they will be selling greater varieties of products, ranging from clothes and accessories to toys for kids. They are even planning to offer IT related products at their supermarket stores. Moreover, he has a plan to open a new Hearty Mart retail outlet at Charottar, the proposal of which is currently under consideration of the franchiser group. Vadgam franchisee is even interested in opening a restaurant under the banner of Hearty Mart in its locality. Earlier, it was not clear whether this kind of an idea would be approved by the franchiser group, but Vadgam franchisee was enthusiastic about the project and kept requesting the franchisers to allow him to open a restaurant. Nadeem has finally valued his idea and has permitted the opening of restaurant just next to the supermarket store. He told us that the next time we visit Vadgam, he would be happy to serve us from the restaurant just adjacent to the supermarket store.

Dholka franchisee reported that, along with retail business, they would like to start a wholesale dealership in collaboration with the HME with an objective of catering to the needs of the local retailers. Jethipura and Surat franchisees are interested in opening new retail outlets in new locations with more variety of goods. Also, Meta franchisee likes to expand the size of their supermarket. All this indicates that in spite of the fact that they are running their supermarkets in the relatively backward areas, their businesses are moving forward in terms of scalability. The format of supermarket retail at village level which has been initiated by the Hearty Mart group is very unique in kind in India. This model once again proves that retailing in the form of supermarket cannot only be successful in those urban areas where relatively well-to-do people stay, but it can also be a success in villages. However, as we can understand, while entrepreneurs would not generally want to look at the village markets for such projects due to very limited scope of scalability, the Hearty Mart initiative has moved forward with its social objective of catering to the desires of the village people and changing their lifestyle, without indulging in any kind of non-commercial approach. In this regard, we can cite the example of Dholka franchisee. Earlier, he had a very small shop in a village and the customer base was very limited. After he had joined Hearty Mart as a franchisee, his general store got a new outlook (i.e. supermarket outlook) and, due to its various policies of accommodating poor customers, it became much popular in the surrounding villages within a couple of years' time. Currently, as the franchisee reported, people from 26 surrounding villages visit his supermarket store.

This has been again reiterated by Wajir Ali (a partner of Nadeem) who said that Hearty Mart wants to make profit and grow, but, at the same time, it wants to share the benefits of the organisation with as many people as it can. Wajir told that they want to make Hearty Mart to be a big and popular brand so that they can share the increased benefits with the downtrodden. He told that the organisation believes in the philosophy of 'growth of all'. According to Wajir, the owners of the Hearty Mart do not want to increase the bank balance without any cause; rather, they want to rear their business as a child and take care of every member who is associated with it—be it an employee or a customer.

Charismatic and Visionary Leader, and Strong, Committed and Value-driven Management Team

Finding franchisees for organised retail store (e.g. supermarket) in rural areas was a challenging task for Nadeem who is the franchiser of the Hearty Mart group. In general, convincing rural investors (who have very low capital base) for such projects may be found to be difficult unless some successful models do already exist in practice. In this regard, Nadeem has an advantage over many other entrepreneurs in the sense that he belongs to the family of the head of the Chilea sect. This has given him an opportunity to influence the investment decisions of his religious followers. As a real entrepreneur with some social views, he grabbed the opportunity and set a vision of doing business with his rural counterparts in order to bring in some changes in rural Gujarat.

Before he started this franchising initiative, he had been well placed in a Mumbai based advertising company. Nadeem could have continued his advertising job and thus led his life otherwise, because he was not unhappy with the pay he was getting. But, Nadeem could foresee the opportunity of new business through his Chilea community networks. And, at the same time, he thought that people of the community could also benefit through a new business opportunity. This way, his thinking showed him the way of earning profit margin on the one hand, and also showed the way of helping community people on the other. Moreover, while he had been looking for a new business opportunity, he could have set-up a small-scale business unit. But, he indulged himself in opening a business in somewhat large-scale in which he would be able to engage greater number of people. A franchisee-based supermarket model was a relatively large business concept for Nadeem. It is known that a supermarket model involves forward as well as backward linkage mechanisms. That means, in the forward integration, there is some scope for engaging some people in the logistics and the related activities, whereas, in the backward integration, several manufacturing activities can be encouraged.

Nadeem says that he holds the position of a leader and the foremost quality of a leader is to grow the ability of leadership within every member of a team. He has floated a FDC (franchisee development cell) to look after different issues of his franchisees. It is a group or a forum where all the franchisees as well as franchiser meet to discuss the daily problems and look for optimal solutions. Finally, the minutes of the meeting are shared with every franchisee. Being a member of the Chilea community's sect-head family, Nadeem could have easily maintained a hierarchical position within the larger Hearty Mart organisation. But, instead, he followed a participatory approach. His vision is to go together, not alone. The participatory approach is a part of the reflection of that vision. Besides, Nadeem acts more like a friend, mentor and philosopher than a franchiser. He knows that almost all his franchisees are educationally lagging behind and have traditional outlook. With such background, it is difficult for them to go forward as far as modern format of franchisee-based supermarket business is concerned. Modern franchisers will hardly allow franchisees of such backward background to collaborate with them. Nadeem knows their limitations and continuously guide them accordingly so that they can cope up with fast changing modern outlook of the current time. Along with profit, social change is one of the objectives of Nadeem. He could have himself opened up Hearty Mart retail outlets in the locations where the franchisee retail outlets are currently located and scale up his margins with the help of more professional people and staff. But he wanted to move forward with his community people who would have otherwise got no better opportunity. He wanted to serve his community through the betterment of his franchisees, workforce engaged in the larger Hearty Mart organisation, and the customers.

Another burning example is found from the career history of Wajir Ali who is now a very active partner of Nadeem Jafri. In his interview, Wajir Ali told that he had started his career as a cleaning boy in his uncle's restaurant at Sarkhej. He moved up to manning the restaurant desk, though he was not happy with that work and, a few years later, he started his own restaurant with very small amount of capital. But, unfortunately, it did not work well as it was expected and, as a consequence of it, he fell into deep losses. He decided to switch to other business and thus he started trading *papad*, where he would buy it from the trader and sell it to the various markets under the banner of his cottage enterprise, namely Ashish enterprise. He used to sell it to households and village shops. Later, he started selling some spices along with Papad to Chilea restaurants with sheer intention of expansion of market. His financial condition improved marginally. Later, he joined hands with a local pickle supplier, who agreed to share his pickle business with him if he takes the charge of marketing in the areas where he sells his papad and spices. In return, the person agreed that he will market his papad and spices in the areas where he sell his pickles. When he agreed to his terms, he had three products in his kitty, but the profit was very nominal; especially Wajir Ali was not satisfied with it. He had no other option but to continue. He used to supply these three products to far off villages, no matter small or big. Since these villages had no good connectivity or infrastructure, at times it so happened that his products would get spoilt, especially during rainy season (due to water logging or heavy rainfall). By the time he reaches the place to deliver papad, he comes to know that they have been wet and no more of use. He used to bear lots of losses in rainy season. Anyway, he had to work very hard for the purpose of marketing of his products. Meanwhile the pickle business owner vested out of the business and sold the entire business. While he was struggling a lot in his life, Nadeem offered him the post of manager at the HME, looking at his good experience of marketing in rural Gujarat. In less than one year time, Nadeem took him as a partner of Hearty Mart. Wajir admitted that this proposal was like a blessing for him. He immediately agreed and joined Nadeem's hands. Wajir remarked that it was not like one plus one; rather he felt this integration as 11. This expresses how happy he was, after Nadeem pulled him up and placed him in the domain of the Hearty Mart organisation as a partner. Since Wajir has experience of travelling in the villages while he used to supply his papad to the village shops, Nadeem gave him the responsibility of HME which, as described earlier, functions like a supplier to the Hearty Mart franchisees and Chilea restaurants, among others. Thus, Nadeem picked up a needy but right person for an important work.

Nadeem understood that Gujarat has been growing faster on industrial front than many other states in India, and thus he intended to take benefit of such growth of Gujarat. He thought that it was not proper to deviate from the overall growth trajectory; rather it could be beneficial if one attempts to ride on it. Nadeem also understands that to take the advantage of growth, one has to be equipped in terms of education and skill. He is himself a well-educated person and believes in pulling his associates to higher level and hence, he encourages his partners and colleagues to be educated. He has encouraged Wajir Ali to complete his graduation and to follow a spoken English course in order to improve his communication skill. Having been inspired by Nadeem, Wajir has enrolled himself for a couple of programmes at Ahmedabad along with his staff members to follow a training programme on marketing and, for this, all the costs were borne by Hearty Mart. Nadeem has also made him registered at Business Network India, an online pool of small and medium innovative entrepreneurs, where they share their ideas and help each other in case they need any assistance relating to the local markets. Nadeem has employed three MBA graduates (Deepak, Nitin and Snehal). They do not only work for the operational matters, but also educate and train other employees on various operational skills since Nadeem wants them to do this in order to raise the level of skill of most of his employees. Wajir Ali invites marketing executives from big companies to share their insights on market with his sales staff and also to train them on various sales tactics.

All the franchisees of Nadeem belong to small villages. They might have conservative upbringing but being associated with Nadeem, they are all very enthusiasts to see the world around and to step out of their closed environment. One thing which we noted as external evaluators is that though they are from conservative background, none of them is rigid. Though they are conventional, they are willing to adopt and learn new modern ideas and tactics and are open to change. For an instance, Nadeem is soon going to introduce online system where the franchisee will be updating his daily turnover which will in turn help the franchiser and the HME for future procurement and every franchisee will be on constant watch of performance. So far after joining Hearty Mart, every franchisee has mentioned that there is an upgradation in their standard of living. Hearty Mart has given them exposure to the outer world, for which their confidence level has increased and they are growing as active and dynamic franchisees.

Some Islamic Influences

During interviews, the franchisees of Hearty Mart told that in their business, they follow certain ethics that have been underlined by their religion and which is manifested in *Hadith*. For example, the Vadgam franchisee told that business is something which is very sacred to him, and thus he is ready to take back a product from a customer if the customer is not satisfied with the same even after partial use. The Surat and the Dholka franchisee told that business is itself a religious activity to them, and thus they weigh their every commercial activity on the religious scale. In the line of this ethical thinking, almost all franchisees told that they do not believe in cheating, selling poor quality goods or inferior goods, and looking for undesirably high profit margins. All the stakeholders of Hearty Mart do make contributions for *Zakat* as social responsibility.[2] But, one of them has different concept. For an instance, Dholka franchisee says that once he has paid the royalty to the franchiser it is the franchiser's duty to pay the *Zakat*. However, Vadgam franchisee does pay *Zakat* as he thinks that it is his duty. Other franchisees such as Pipodar and Kanai, however, are very religious persons and pay *Zakat* and talk about it with full enthusiasm.

---

2. *Zakat* is a form of obligatory religious tax in Islam. It is based on income and the value of all of one's possessions. It is customarily 2.5 per cent of a Muslim's total income, savings and wealth above a minimum amount known as *nisab*, but Islamic scholars differ on how much nisab is and other aspects of zakat. The collected amount is paid first to zakat collectors, and then it goes to poor Muslims, to new converts to Islam, to Islamic clergy, and others.

Conclusion

In this chapter, we have studied the social aspects of the Hearty Mart supermarket franchising business model. In the light of some important pillars of social entrepreneurship (as stated above), we have studied the role of Nadeem and the role of Hearty Mart in initiating some changes in some rural areas of Gujarat. Our findings suggest that Nadeem has played a pioneering role in facilitating the setting up of supermarket-style retail outlets in rural Gujarat and thereby allowing rural poor to experience modern shopping at their localities within their affordability. Hearty Mart has customer base of low and lower-middle income groups and thus, its main objective has been to serve them with the best available quality at the lowest available prices. Also, Nadeem's initiative motivated some villagers of farming community to join his hands as franchisees and build a strong franchising network. This has created further opportunity of employment for the local, rural, unemployed youth in the rural retail supermarkets. More importantly, the franchiser and the franchisees are not seen to be doing any philanthropy; they are following efficiently the market principles and thus their scalability is not being hindered. Through the help of various mechanisms (as stated above), the franchisees are selling products at discounted prices and this is helping them to excel in terms of scalability.

6

Behavioural, Institutional and Organisational Responses of the Hearty Mart Franchiser and Franchisees

Introduction

In this chapter, we have tried to understand the Hearty Mart franchising framework through our direct conversation with the franchiser and the franchisees. As we have indicated earlier, Hearty Mart can be regarded as a model of hybrid form which stands somewhere between 'market' and 'organisation'. It is operating and functioning in the market; but since market is not the solution to all the economic problems, the franchising model which builds on a coordination mechanism within a new organisational framework at the backdrop of rural-urban duality is the focus of the discussion of this chapter. Both the franchiser and the franchisee deal with several things for which they opt for market transaction. But, setting up of supermarkets—even in small scale—in the rural areas by the rural Chilea entrepreneurs would have been extremely difficult if Nadeem, the franchiser, had not joined their hands. Thus, coordination (and cooperation) between franchiser and franchisee plays an important role in this model. In this chapter, our aim is to understand this model from the perspective of a new development that has taken place based on the organisational and institutional coordination in some rural areas of Gujarat.

A Supermarket Format in Rural Setting

Analysing all the interviews of the franchisees which have been conducted by us, we can say that the franchisees operate and function in an environment (in villages, in this case) in which various socio-cultural groups are interacting. The approach of these franchising communities (mainly the Chileas) to the larger external environment seems to be conservative, and so, a large-scale franchising model is difficult to be comprehended by the entrepreneurs of such groups. In many cases, the franchisees and the customers, as we found during field survey, are both from poor background and mainly from the rural/semi-urban cultural environment. It was difficult to set up a 'modern' retail store in a locality where population had an experience of being exposed only to very limited, traditional grocery shops. Similarly, for the customers of rural setting, the issue of familiarity with modern retail or supermarket was a concern. That is why Nadeem thought of a community-based franchising system which would address these issues. For an instance, a forward thinking and unconventional franchisee of Hearty Mart such as Asad Khan Pathan of Vadgam Store told us that he, as an entrepreneur, wanted to change the conventional format of retail stores and shopping behaviour of customers of his locality. This has been possible after joining hands of Nadeem.

Organisation, Coordination and Motivation

A fundamental observation about the economic world is that people can produce more if they cooperate, specialising in their productive activities and then transacting with one another. The role of organisation is important because specialised producers need to trade, and thus their decisions and actions need to be coordinated to achieve the gains of cooperation through the help of an organisation such as Hearty Mart. And, the producer or traders must be motivated to carry out their roles in the cooperative activity.

In the context of Hearty Mart, when the franchising model was initiated at a store at Ilol, there was no management 'team' in place at that time. In fact, only Nadeem Jafri was responsible for the entire coordination. As the Hearty Mart model grew, the coordination process became very complicated. Hence, let us now provide an organisational chart of the entire Hearty Mart system so that we can understand it in simple manner (see Figure 6.1). As shown at the top of Figure 6.1, there are two bodies—centralised decision-making

Figure 6.1

Organisational Chart of Hearty Mart

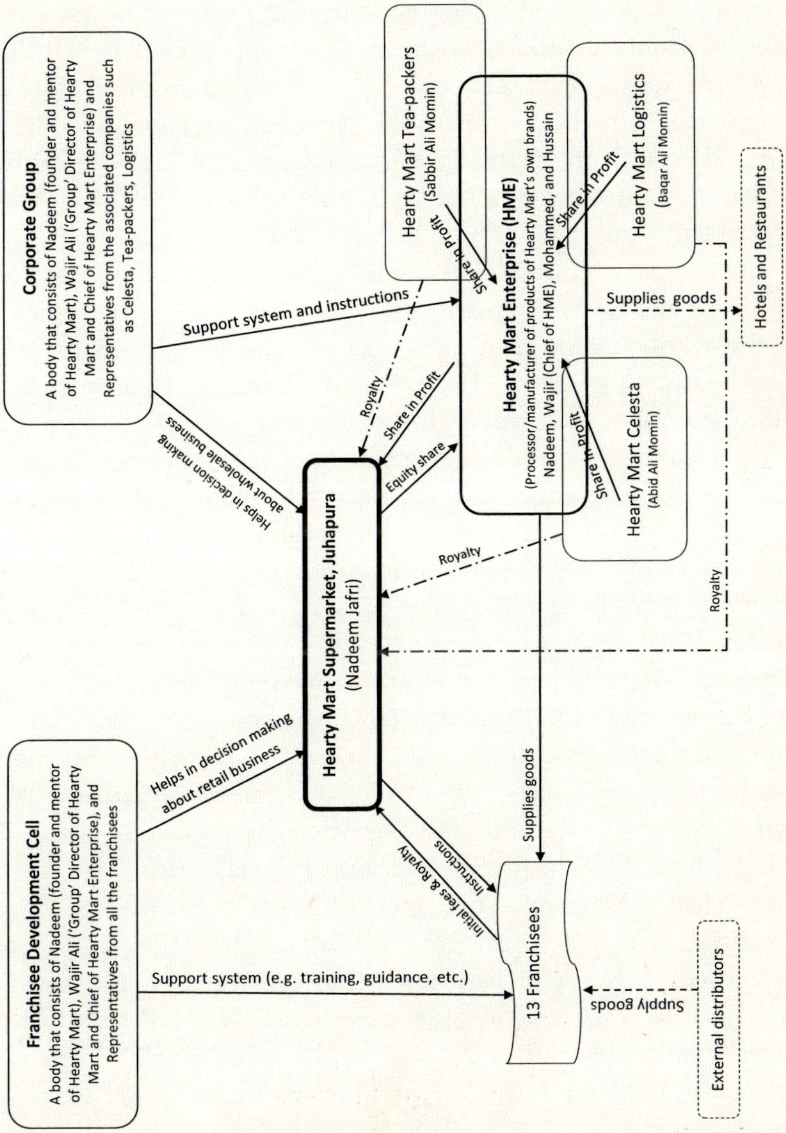

Source: By authors (based on field survey).

core group called 'CG (corporate group)' (which consists of the key decision makers such as Nadeem himself, Wajir Ali who is the chief of HME, and representatives from the associated companies such as Hearty Mart Celesta, Hearty Mart Tea-Packers and Hearty Mart Logistics) and the 'FDC (franchisee development cell)' (which consists of people such as Nadeem, Wajir Ali and representatives from all the franchisees). In this context, the response we have got during the interviews with the franchisees made us realise that the centralised decision-making process has been able to facilitate the operational part of the Hearty Mart Franchising system.

As regards, centralised decision-making process, let us first clarify one thing very clearly. The CG takes care of the issues as far as the wholesale marketing of various products of Hearty Mart's own brand (e.g. HME, Hearty Mart Celesta, Hearty Mart Tea-Packers, etc.) is concerned. The FDC takes care of the issues as far as the retail marketing strategies of the Hearty Mart franchisees are concerned (See Figure 6.1 for a detailed understanding about these issues). As we see in the figure, four organisations have been placed over the right hand side bottom corner that includes HME, Hearty Mart Celesta, Hearty Mart Tea-packers and Hearty Mart Logistics. Hearty Mart Supermarket at Juhapura (i.e. Nadeem) gets its share of profit (as per its equity share) from HME since Nadeem is the partner of the latter. Similarly, HME gets its profit share (as per its equity share) from Celesta, tea-packers and Logistics, because HME has partnership with other three associated companies. Why do then Celesta, Tea-Packers and Logistics pay royalty to Hearty Mart Juhapura Unit? As Nadeem said, these three entities use the brand name 'Hearty Mart' and that is why they pay the royalty.

What is the role of HME as far as the 13 franchisees are concerned? Observe in Figure 6.1 that there is an arrow from HME towards the franchisees. This indicates that HME supplies goods (which are processed and packaged by HME itself,[1] Hearty Mart Celesta and Hearty Mart Tea-packers) to Hearty Mart Franchisees.

1. HME itself is engaged in processing (e.g. packaging) and supply of its own products such as Basmati rice, spices, sauces, dry fruits, etc. to hotels and restaurants, and to the retail franchisees of Hearty Mart. For further details of the products supplied by HME, Hearty Mart Celesta and Hearty Mart Tea-packers, see Chapter – 2.

Note that HME also supplies goods to the hotels and restaurants (mentioned in the right-hand bottom of Figure 6.1). Hearty Mart Logistics carries out all this supply related work. However, the franchisees also procure goods from the external distributors/ suppliers (mentioned in the left-hand bottom corner in Figure 6.1). It is not mandatory for them to procure goods from the Hearty Mart. If the same products are available in the market at very reasonable prices as compared to the prices offered by the HME and its other associated companies, why should the franchisees buy products from the Hearty Mart?

This freedom given to the Hearty Mart franchisees is instrumental for their growth. In this perspective, what is the specific usefulness of setting up a system of supplying some goods or items by HME to the franchisees? In those cases where the coordination mechanism in a formalised contract is successful as in the case of Gujarat Cooperative Milk Marketing Federation (GCMMF), the structure is based on assuring committed supply. The fundamental thing is that such organisations want to ensure uninterrupted supply of products to their customers. And this can be ensured by a good procurement system. GCMMF ensures regular procurement of milk from dairy farmers in order to maintain continued supply of their final products (Chandra and Tirupati 2003). Similarly, one of the objectives of the Hearty Mart supply mechanism is to ensure the supply of some specific items to its franchisees.

Let us now conclude the earlier discussion. Does the Hearty Mart group strictly follow the centralised decision-making process through the creation of FDC and CG? However, Hearty Mart does not follow an entirely centralised decision-making process. Many decisions are taken at the franchisee level as well. A considerable degree of autonomy has been given to them and the system has been made quite flexible.

Another important aspect of the organisation is the 'chain of commands'. Figure 6.2 shows the chain of commands within Hearty Mart. Nadeem is the chief mentor of the entire Hearty Mart organisation. As already said above, the FDC takes care of the issues relating to the franchisees and CG takes care of the issues relating to the associated companies engaged in wholesale marketing. By two arrows—one between Nadeem and the FDC and the other between Nadeem and the CG—it is indicated in Figure 6.2 that Nadeem directs the FDC and the CG about holding the meetings of these two bodies. The decisions that are taken by the FDC and the CG are then passed on to Wajir Ali (Group Director) for execution (two arrows—one between FDC and Wajir Ali and the other between CG and Wajir Ali—indicates this in Figure 6.2). Then Wajir Ali carries out his responsibility in collaboration with the franchisees and the wholesale groups. The dotted arrows—one between FDC and franchisees and the other between CG and wholesale group—indicate some direct communications (not via Wajir Ali). For example, some skilled or trained FDC members (either Nadeem or Wajir or someone else) or some person invited by the FDC provides some training or consultancy to the franchisees. Similar is true for the direct relation between the CG and the wholesale group.

Decision-making and Coordination

In this context, Nadeem has his own insight. We have said above that the coordination at Hearty Mart in the initial stage was taken care of by Nadeem himself. That is, the initial franchising relationship grew under his close scrutiny. But, as the number of franchisees increased with time, the complexity of the group grew and, as said earlier, the FDC was formed for making coordination more streamlined, more organised and more formal. We asked Nadeem about the coordination mechanism between Hearty Mart Juhapura and the franchisees/other units. Is it guided by the FDC, or is coordination still maintained with the help of personalised guidance of Nadeem? In this context, Nadeem answered that all the franchisees come under the FDC and follow the rules formulated by it. The issues raised by any unit are taken care of without any discrimination and all the franchisees are given guidance on the basis of need. Further, the franchisees are regularly in touch with him regarding various matters. For example, price is such an issue which needs to be carefully handled because expansion of market often depends on prices of commodities. Nadeem's experience is

Figure 6.2

Chain of Commands in Hearty Mart

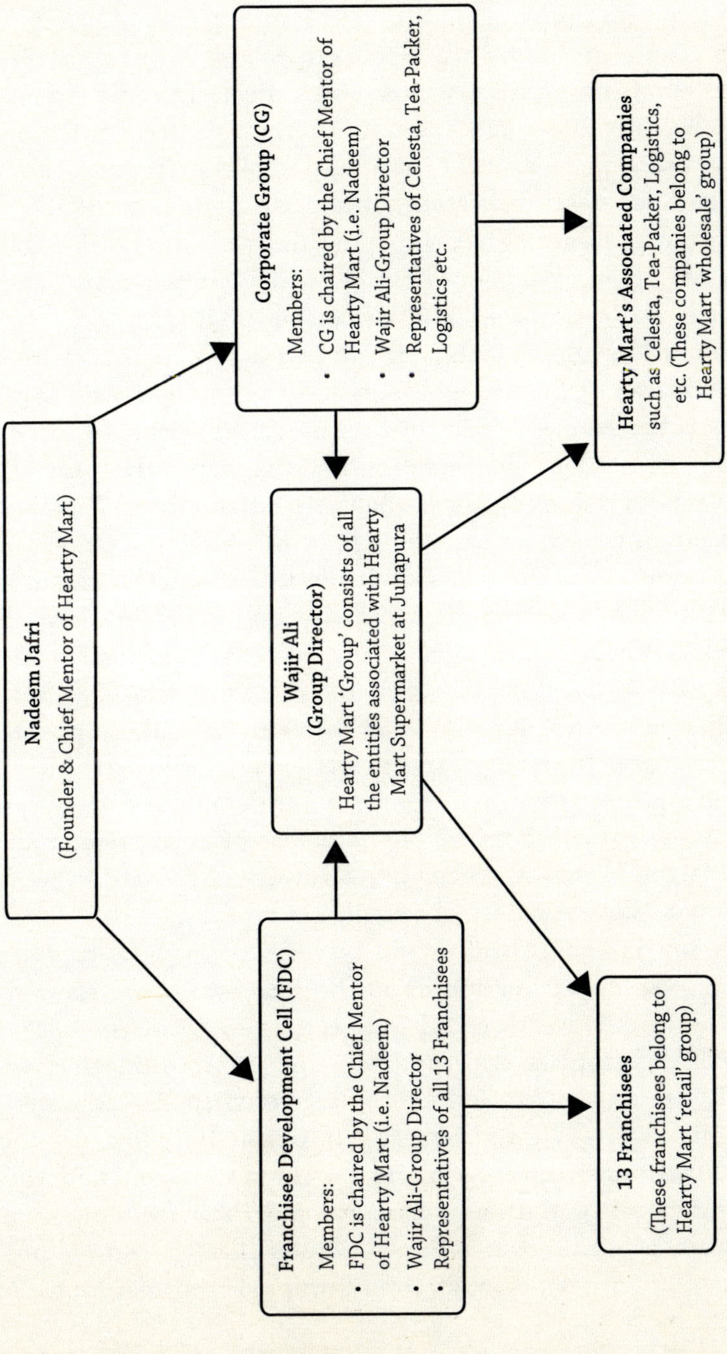

Source: By authors (based on field survey).

instrumental in deciding about prices. Thus, the franchisees often call him up for opinions on different issues including prices. Besides, many issues/problems are discussed in the meeting of FDC, and sorted out through discussions. This reflects the phenomenon that when decentralised process fails to yield desired outcome, some decisions are made with the intervention of central authority in order to strengthen decentralisation rather than to undermine it.

As far as Hearty Mart Juhapura unit is concerned, Sabbir Bhai plays key role in decision-making process. It is worth noting that Sabbir is no franchisee; he is a manager at Hearty Mart Juhapura. According to Nadeem, Sabbir is not just a good manager but he has all the quality of an entrepreneur; and they enjoy good coordination between themselves. He also told us that everyday they do meet for half-an-hour in the morning for discussing the pros and cons of various decisions taken by Sabbir particularly in the absence of Nadeem. However, since Sabbir Bhai takes the sole responsibility of management of Juhapura Unit of Hearty Mart, Nadeem is given opportunity to spend enough time for taking care of various issues related to the franchisees. Especially, Nadeem makes extra efforts for the growth of two franchisees, namely Veda and Idar, as both these franchisees are not growing well in terms of making profit. While Veda is a new franchisee and needs time to take-off, Idar is a bit difficult case for Nadeem. Nadeem is a little apprehensive about Idar franchisee's growth because of the deficit of entrepreneurship skills of the latter. However, during our fieldwork of this study, we came to know that Idar franchisee has finally shut down.

As far as the coordination is concerned, how do we assess Nadeem? From the version of all the franchisees, we came to know that Nadeem provides equal importance to all of them. Nadeem's style of developing coordination and communication with his franchisees is unique and this is reflected in the answers of the franchisees interviewed by us. We found the 'personal touch' in his coordination approach. He has never encroached the areas of responsibility of the franchisees and their freedom of making decisions. What is interesting to note is that Nadeem is pushing a formal/modern idea through the traditional/informal route. This has been precisely possible for two reasons. One, Nadeem is a qualified management graduate and has also gained experience in corporate sector, especially in the advertisement media. Two, Nadeem is culturally rooted into villages through close religious ties with his community acquaintances, as has been mentioned earlier. It seems that such blending of two factors (modern and traditional) has perhaps been the key to Nadeem's success in franchising business. The role of Nadeem as a good coordinator has been proved in FDC meetings. For example, Vadgam franchisee once raised an issue in an FDC meet that there should be uniformity in the promotional offers (e.g. rates of discounts on various items) made by all the franchisees. But this issue is a bit complicated owing to the reason that a centrally regulated approach in such matter has a possibility to undermine the importance of a village franchisee's locally rooted sentiments which are often taken into consideration in local marketing approach. To tackle this issue, Nadeem divided promotional offers into two categories: one is the central promotional offers while the other includes local promotional offers undertaken by the franchisee according to local and/or seasonal festivals. It has been decided that central promotional schemes would be attached to the items that are procured by franchisees via HME, whereas the local promotional offers are attached to those items that are procured by the franchisees themselves.

In Hearty Mart, responsibilities have been distributed to several people as far as addressing of queries made by the franchisees is concerned. For instance, any queries regarding the market are addressed by Wajir Ali; the issues related to discounts/offers are also dealt with by Wajir Ali; the need for training (e.g. management, marketing, etc.) is addressed by the FDC; and strategic and informal queries are addressed by Nadeem. Nadeem's guidance has been proved to be crucial in several cases. For instance, Nadeem's guidance on issues like when to move fast, when to move slowly, when to expand etc. has been important. Crucial decision-making in business should generate from the process of enriching experiences, and not from any sudden reactions. As Nadeem reports, the Ilol franchisee is well groomed now, after receiving guidance on a regular basis in the last eight years and can think more dexterously about his business.

Wajir Ali, within HME, has organised very well the integration of all economic and management related activities. His staff has been well informed of all related matters and well equipped too. For instance, if he is not present in the office but an issue related to finance has cropped up, Snehal is there to take the decision. In case, HME falls short of staff in one department—for example, in packing department—then staff members go for internal shift. May be, someone from administration department takes the responsibility, and thus none of the activities are hampered in case of non-availability of staff or absenteeism because their specialised grooming has taught them to adopt such flexibility. At HME, every individual has their own dignified place which is worth counting. Coordination is the part of culture of the organisation. As Wajir Ali told us, he is managing the entire HME; but, when it comes to interpreting the daily MIS (management information system), he seeks help from Deepak (manager at HME). Hearty Mart as a corporate house is prodigious example of several small but interesting consolidations of activities performed at different levels.

The Motivation Factor and Opportunity

Nadeem had been doing a job before he started his Hearty Mart Supermarket at Juhapura, and consequently the franchising ventures. As he reported, he used to be paid handsome salary in his job. Then, why did he take to entrepreneurship where there was no assurance of the returns and no guarantee that he would be successful? It was a huge step, for a salaried professional to give-up the high paying job and to start up a new venture. Taking a decision of moving from a relatively secured job to self-employment is not always very easy, especially because of the fact that Nadeem was not aware of the tits and bits of the franchising business. Further, entrepreneurship involves risk of failures, especially when the entrepreneur lacks proper knowledge about his proposed business. Factor such as competition with well-established brands further hikes the level of risk. While he was aware of all these limitations, what is it that motivated Nadeem?

Let us try to explain this. Gujarat is a traditionally developed state in India. Besides, growth of the non-primary sector (industry and service) has been accelerated in last one decade. The cities and towns of Gujarat in recent years have experienced fast growth of various services including modern retail (or organised retail). Such fast growth has also taken place in Ahmedabad city. However, within Ahemadabad, there are several pockets where growth of organised retail has not been experienced. Juhapura area is one of them and, as a potential entrepreneur, Nadeem could find some opportunity waiting for him. Later, his success proved that his decision of switching from job to entrepreneurship was correct. Initially his Juhapura based unit was not growing very well. He started his supermarket in 2004, whereas he started earning moderate returns since 2007. Since he was experiencing limited growth due to his limited capital strength as well as low profile promotional activities, he adopted the idea of franchising to expand market and to scale up his capital base by taking the opportunity of his close links with Chilea Community as already described in previous chapters. Actually he got the idea of Franchisee model from his friend Hemant Trivedi who was a professor at Mudra Institute of Communication, Ahmedabad (MICA). Besides, he went through several relevant books to study supermarket franchisee model and also collected information from various sources. To study various aspects of franchisee business, he visited several exhibitions where big franchisers were looking for their new franchisees. Hence, his personal ambition was his main motivation for opening Hearty Mart.

The Partner

How was Wajir Ali, the partner in HME, motivated to join Nadeem's venture. Two factors influenced his inclusion in Hearty Mart. One, Wajir was looking for help to further expand and grow while he was running his own company, Ashish Enterprise. He was facing obstacles due to his formal management skill deficit. On the other hand, Nadeem was looking for a person who might not have formal management qualification but have practical exposure of supply chain business (e.g. supplying materials to hotels). Also, Wajir was highly influenced by Nadeem's positive attitude and his family's religious values. As far as modern attitude and religious values are concerned, Wajir had a different view before he met Nadeem. He used to believe that religion and business cannot go hand in hand. Nadeem made him understand that there is no conflict between business and religion; rather, some aspects of religion can be very well implemented in business. In addition to all this, social motivation did also play some role for Wajir Ali, which we have discussed in the empirical chapter of social entrepreneurship.

Property Rights and Transaction Costs in the Hearty Mart Franchising System

In Hearty Mart, the franchiser and the franchisees are maintaining a loose relationship. For example, there is no legal contract between the franchiser and the franchisee. Do the franchisees feel secure with the informal contract? In the interview of Sadiq Ali at Dholka, we came to know that he feels very secure about his contract. In the absence of formal contract, trust based on socio-cultural religious ties among the individuals of the community is conceived as a form of contract by the parties involved in Hearty Mart. They have full faith in such contract. In this case, such contract seems to be more powerful than a legal contract, since the individuals put a greater weight to their religious organisation than to a formal contract. If a contract leads to exercising property rights over the terms and conditions of a business, the franchisees, in this case, did not express any insecurity about their property right at the time of interview. We will be discussing this in further detail later in this chapter.

However, in this context, an important observation may be made. Both the franchiser and the franchisee may be experiencing low transaction cost or nil transaction cost due to the absence of formal contract. The reason is that transaction costs are often the costs that arise when individuals exchange ownership rights to economic assets and enforce their exclusive rights. "The fundamental idea of transaction costs is that they consist of the cost of arranging a contract ex-ante and monitoring and enforcing it ex-post..." (Matthews 1986). Since trust is an important component in the

Hearty Mart model, the franchiser and the franchisees felt almost no need for arranging a contract and consequently the need for monitoring a contract did not arise at all.

Another point is important as far as organisational aspects are concerned. In order to cut small retail outlets on price with economies of scale, formalised retail chains such as Reliance Fresh are working towards more contractual organisational mechanisms in terms of both ensuring timely procurement as well as quality of produce. Hearty Mart has rather adopted a flexible system. As said earlier, the franchisees can procure goods from HME or from open market/distributor or from both. To maintain the supply uninterrupted, the franchisee can choose any option. There is no contractual organisational mechanism in this regard. Thus, since there was no formal agreement, no legal procedure was followed. Eventually, this has saved all the franchising parties from incurring additional financial costs. In other words, we can say that this has saved them from bearing some transaction costs.

However, these costs can be analysed as the costs of dealings with regard to their property/assets with various agents in different socio-cultural environments in village or town. For example, the Dholka franchisee has a considerable number of Jain customers in his locality, due to which he has refrained from keeping frozen foods at his superstore (since Jain people do not consume items that are kept in refrigerator in supermarket). These kinds of instances, which reflect different transaction costs in different social environments (the supermarket has to procure certain fresh items on daily basis and this creates some additional transaction costs), are relevant for making important decisions in the business.

As far as the contracting relationship at Hearty Mart is concerned, both the franchiser and the franchisee, as we said, are involved in informal contracts. The franchisee obtains, as already said, the right to use a brand name owned by the franchiser for a royalty fee, though only half per cent on turnover. This is a market transaction in the absence of secured system in Hearty Mart. However, the franchisee is an entrepreneur who invests in his own establishment. The franchiser and the franchisee are regarded as two separate organisations in one system. But they have a common brand name which is an important asset for all the parties involved in Hearty Mart. The brand name really matters when an organisation has earned reputation in the market. What if some dispute arises in the future in Hearty Mart in connection with the brand name?

During the fieldwork, as indicated above, we have found that no formal agreement has been made between the franchiser and the franchisee and they do not possess any legal paper regarding their tie-up. This means, the rights over the brand name called 'Hearty Mart' are not secured from the either side. If any disputes arise in this regard in the future, then the situation may lead to legal complications. For example, a question might arise as to whose brand it is. More precisely, who is the owner of the brand and who is lending it to whom? Moreover, if the brand name is not registered in favour of Nadeem Jafri then it can be snatched by any franchisee or even by a third party. Similarly, in absence of any formal contract, the franchiser may also ask a franchisee to give up the brand name if their relationship is not cordial at any point in time in the future, avoiding any legal complications. However, as far as the rights over physical capital such as the assets owned by franchiser and franchisees are concerned, question of violation of exercising the choice over property or capital does not arise. This is because there is no overlapping area between the franchiser and franchisee in terms of occupying property.

What does Nadeem say about the possibility of emergence of future disputes? Nadeem, as we have felt from his version during interviews, is not bothered about it at all. Why is Nadeem not worried or bothered? The reason is that the social or religious or the community institution is so strongly present in this franchisee framework that legal or formal contract seems to be unnecessary or irrelevant. Rather, the introduction of formality in this case might hurt the sentiments of the parties involved, because such sentiments are attached with the community bonding. Thus, nobody wants to propose for a formal contract because each of the members who are involved thinks that signing a formal contract is rather equivalent to nurturing some distrust in the mind about Nadeem. Hence, no one is in a position to have doubts about his business tie with others.

In terms of property rights, as discussed in the interviews with the franchisees, we saw the face of coin from the franchisees' side. The fact is that although the contract between Nadeem and franchisees is loose in nature, all parties are quite secure about the (informal) contract. Our inquisitiveness multiplied and we asked Nadeem a question pertaining to the contract while interviewing him. In reply, Nadeem told us that he is much secured about the contract and other rights related to property (e.g. his brand name) due to close religious connection between the franchiser and the franchisee. Thus, can one think that in the absence of formal contract, there is a possibility that a franchisee might break the relationship with Nadeem at any point in time in future and snatch the brand name? According to Nadeem, the chance of this seems to be very remote due to their religious bonding between each other. Moreover, as a member of the family of the religious leader, Nadeem is more interested to get his franchisees involved in the 'process' of supermarket business than to 'unnecessarily' get them involved in a formal contract and such other legal complications. Let us explain this further. The customer often faces limitations during his shopping at local grocery shop, because the grocery shop often suffers from limited choice over a range of a particular product (i.e. it does not store many varieties of brands of a product). For example, toothpaste or shampoo of various ranges are produced by different manufacturers, whereas a grocery shop or general store may not go for all the ranges, and this often restricts a customer to opt for his purchasing decision from the given limited varieties. Hence, a supermarket which provides larger varieties has a competitive advantage over the general store or grocery shop. This is just a part of modern retail format. Nadeem has taught this to his village level franchisees as a part of the 'process' of the modern retail marketing. The reason for opting for larger varieties is not just to satisfy customer's differential choices but also to cater to various income groups.

As regards contract between franchiser and franchisee, let us mention an interesting facet of it. Apart from the religious bonding, another factor also needs to be mentioned. Since most of the franchisees have hardly gone through primary level of education, the present achievement—whatever they have achieved so far through Nadeem's initiatives—has added a different dimension to their lives. So, Nadeem does not think, as he has conveyed, that the franchisees are really bothered about formal contract. Another factor is that rural uneducated common people are usually averse to get to legal system and hence they are disinclined towards signing a legal contract. Citing all these reasons, Nadeem has told us that he never asked the franchisees to go for a contract. Another interesting point is that several types of scrutiny may be undertaken during the process of legalisation which, as Asad Khan Pathan (a franchisee) has said, might not leave enough room for freedom to work at their ease.

However, although the contract is informal, there is not much obligation from the franchisees' side since Nadeem takes half percent royalty on annual turnover from the franchisees. And, as far as franchisees are concerned, they feel that their future with Hearty Mart depends on their capacity to grow with brand Hearty Mart. According to franchisees like Sadiq Ali at Dholka, sky is the limit to grow with this brand. He says that he is willing to expand his business. He is planning to take up distributorship of HME. He says that he will continue to go with this business until end of his life. This shows that there is complete confidence among franchisees about Hearty Mart.

As defined in chapter 4, a limited awareness of the franchisees regarding knowledge of external environment gives occurrence to bounded rationality (Milgrom and Roberts 1992: 127-28). When the external environment is not smoothly and easily accessible for some parties/agents, enacting and enforcing a complete and perfect contract is fraught with problems. In actual transactions, limited foresight caused by restricted exposure, cultural distinctions, the cost of calculating solutions due to very limited education, and the costs of thinking in a planned manner, these are collectively conceptualised as the bounded rationality of the people involved. Where the franchisee is bounded by his limited horizon and approach to outer world, he is bound to follow the leader (here, in this case, the leader is franchiser himself). For example, given the fact that the franchisees in villages find themselves to be lacking in information attributes, it is quite obvious that the faith of franchisees in Nadeem and in the organisation of Hearty Mart has been growing continuously.

Not Sure about Future Problem

The fact that parties/agents in a business model which has been constructed based on informal (even in some formal cases too) contracts may be forced later (after the necessary investments were made) to accept some disadvantageous terms which were not clearly discussed earlier may be termed as the hold-up problem. If a franchisee wants to expand much more than what it is now, then it is expected that the idea could be supported by the franchiser since the Hearty Mart model has grown on the basis of flexible, socio-religious constructs, rather than rigid, formal, contract-bound relationship. Since informalities in various forms play different roles in the Hearty Mart model, freedom enjoyed by the franchisees is an obvious phenomenon in such type of model. But, it is still possible that there will be complications in this model. In a formal contractual model, although several restrictions may be imposed, the contracts often finally comes out as a transparent one where parties involved do not face any deficit of clarity. Contrary to this, parties involved in an informal contract may not be often sure about the future contingencies. They may be apprehensive about the warranty of the fact that there will be no complications in the Hearty Mart model in the future. There are scopes that non-clarity attached to the nature of such informality may even invite introduction of some disadvantageous terms later on. At this moment, we are not sure as to which factor would create the disadvantageous terms later. Is it size of the store, range of products offered, or is it something else? During the field survey, all the franchisees have reported that they are happy with the present form of contract. But, this does not ensure that there will be no problem in the future.

Institutional Trust and Reputation Building

In Hearty Mart organisation, trust is an important factor based on which, as already said, the informal framework of the organisation has grown. This framework provides the 'return' through cooperation. And, such cooperation produces community-specific, distinct, reputation capital as well. As we generally know, a positive reputation earns a company or an organisation long-term competitive advantages. The higher the level of sincere cooperation and trust, the lower the costs for supervising and exercising control (Klewes and Wreschniok 2010). And, the result is that the organisation would gain confidence in meeting the functional and social expectations of a section of people (say Chilea community), on the one hand, and would engage in a process of building a unique identity of itself, on the other.

At the initial phase, it was challenging for Nadeem. Although he belongs to a deeply religious and conservative community, he is an educated open-minded person. But, he knows that most of the people in his community (the Chileas) have personal ambition to grow. Nadeem said to us that he believes in personal growth through educational achievements. And, thus, when he talks about Islamic principles, he does so from the domain of enlightened Islam, meaning that he belongs to both Islamic culture, on the one hand, and modern education-induced enlightenment, on the other. This has been possible for Nadeem because the Chilea community as a whole is usually considered to be of somewhat practical, business minded and liberated mindset. Hence, the result that has been produced so far has experienced a process of quite smooth exchange of ideas between the franchiser and franchisee. Generally speaking, a member of the sect-head family of a community is usually thought to be following very strict religious guidelines. However, as said, Nadeem has gone through modern education. Also, he did not lose the trust in his community members. Similarly, he has also gained support from his followers in favour of his ideas of franchising venture. So, trust has been developed through two-way communications. The Chilea community people (both the franchisees and a section of the customers) did have faith in their sect-head family (and in Nadeem too); and Nadeem was also confident that the village customers would want to accept the new model, especially when India is rapidly urbanising and when consumer culture is changing fast through the intervention of media. These dynamics together has helped Hearty Mart to create and establish a new popular brand. Moreover, the community trust factor has made the transactions within the Hearty Mart System relatively easy and comfortable. This can be a crucial factor for the further growth of the organisation.

We asked Nadeem regarding how confident he was about the growth of brand Hearty Mart. He said that a very few franchisees are having severe problems, while the others are growing very fast. He gave us an instance of two of his franchisees, one of which (located in Vadgam) has been doing extremely well and the other (located in Idar) was finding it difficult to survive and has finally closed down. Both of them have been working in almost same environment and under same mechanism, but due to their differences in attitudes, two different results have occurred.

As indicated earlier, Hearty Mart as a retail supermarket is a very different type of organisation in village areas. Such type of organisation has not yet been flourished in rural India. The form of supermarket differs a lot from the type of existing grocery shops. With the introduction of supermarket in village, the rural customers are getting an exposure to new ambience within the shopping place; and altogether this is giving them a new retail shopping experience in their own locality. The Hearty Mart franchisees maintain a standardised organisational ambience in the same line with the Hearty Mart Juhapura centre. Hence, this provides a modern ambience in the franchisee stores, which is not very common in village India. From the rural organisational point of view, this is an innovative idea. This new organisational framework incorporates a concept which seems to be much better than the organisational concept of general store (*kirana* store). Better in what sense? Let us give an example from what we have experienced during our field visits and interviews. Village general stores are selling shampoos, but Garnier brand is not available. Besides, village shops are selling various *kirana* items, but items such as clothes and shoes are not available. As Nadeem said, unlike general store or grocery shop, Hearty Mart franchisees sell shampoos of most of the renowned brands such as Garnier. Currently, only one franchisee is selling clothes and shoes, but there is possibility that this will be started by the other franchisees as well. In this respect, we can say that Hearty Mart franchisees have dual characteristics. In one sense, they are following a standardised process. And, they also retain considerable amount of autonomy to choose the way of doing their business (e.g. selling additional products such as clothes and shoes).

Issues Related to Information

In a subsistence or semi-subsistence economy in the villages of a developing country, price is often considered to be occupying a prominent place of market mechanism. Price mechanism is an important factor for the Hearty Mart too. However, coordination mechanism plays an important role in the growth of Hearty Mart franchising model. And, we know that coordination is a crucial aspect of organisational economics. Let us now discuss this in further detail. Generally, one may assume that price is one of the main elements of a business system since it implicitly or explicitly bears the information that is required to understand rise and fall of different brands, companies, organisations, or economic activities. That is why solutions to a problem in a semi-subsistence economy are often sought through alteration of prices. In our thesis, we do not wish to say that price is really not an important factor, however, what we would like to emphasise is that alternative solutions do also need to be tapped for prosperity. Moreover, alternative development thinking is crucial because price/market cannot absorb all the information necessary to enable the execution of the transactions. Sometimes, there are fundamental 'information problems' that cannot be resolved by the price system. A number of these problems can, however, be dealt with by means of organisational coordination. Thus, organisations may arise as solutions to information problems. Organisations are sometimes more suited to dealing with certain information problems than are markets where price seems to be central. So, when an individual cannot control the market, he or she can enter into an organisation to reduce the cost of information and communication in order to penetrate into the market. According to Nadeem, organisational process is the underlying factor that has played an important role in the development of the Hearty Mart Franchising model.

Moreover, let us not forget that information asymmetry is a basic problem that prevails in many communities or societies or geographical pockets in India. Such problem may arise due to several reasons, one of which is lack of education which further leads to lack of self-confidence in some individuals. As we found in our fieldwork, the Surat franchisee, due to lack of education, feels shy and is a bit reluctant to communicate frequently with the central leadership of Hearty Mart, including the FDC. We also came to know that he does not frequently communicate with the other franchisees too. Here, the interesting finding we get is that even an organisational strategy as an alternative is not going to yield desired results if some other basic problems (e.g. low level of education) are not properly addressed. We believed that a well developed organisation and its internal network would be found to be a way-out to the problem stated above. As far as most of the franchisees are concerned, the organisation itself appears to be a mechanism to tackle the price-centered information problem. However, the case of Surat franchisee explains that organisational mechanism cannot be proved to be properly functioning if some basic problems such as lack of self-confidence or lack of minimum education are not remedied. This flaw is perhaps associated with the conservative approach of the concerned franchisee owner towards his life and his family. If an actor does not want to extend his human development horizon through the provision of education, he would be trapped into the narrow and conservative social domain and thus would find it difficult to grow. This has been evident from the difference we have found between him and the franchisees as well as associated companies of Hearty Mart such as Asad Khan Pathan, Sadiq Ali, Wajir Ali etc., who have been found to be conceiving liberal as well as practical approach in their life. Hence, there may arise a conflict between the two attitudes—one coming out of conventional ethics and the other coming out of liberal attitudes. If the latter wins then it might be a determining factor for growth of the individual involved.

Another facet of information-related mechanism can be explained through market demands. Usually, the demand in a limited market-base is not unknown to the agents that are operating in the same market. The fluctuations of demand are also known to them. Since the fluctuations depend on the festivities of the communities residing in the area, the franchisees are to handle their stocks and inventories according to the fluctuations in demand. Thus, the local market of the franchisees is dealt with according to the changing needs of the customers in different seasons.

Support System

During interviews, all the franchisees told us that they got proper guidance whenever they had a consultation with the FDC, and they found the guidance useful for them. So, the communication channel between the franchisee and franchiser (franchisees are sharing problems with the centralised body and the centralised body is timely responding to them) is found effective. The effectiveness of such communication channel may be considered as instrumental to the growth of village based franchising model. Since most of the franchisees are not well educated, the FDC's active participation in the regular communication with the franchisees is really required. Nadeem has understood well the significance of the FDC and thus formed it consisting of himself, and some other concerned persons (see Figure 6.1 for the details of the members of the FDC). As said, since there is lack of professionalism as far as the franchisees are concerned, the FDC is filling up the gap through proper guidance. Today's modern organisation and modern marketing approach need professional care which can be facilitated by the FDC. The franchisees know that they have deficiencies, because the world is changing fast and they are unable to cope up with such changes due to lack of their proper education and exposure. It is difficult for Nadeem alone to handle such deficiencies of the franchisees and thus the forming of the FDC was a right decision. Now, consider a situation where information is easily available. Can a less-educated person (for example, Kanai franchisee is 7th standard pass, Pipodar franchisee 10th pass, Dholka franchisee 12th pass, etc.)[2] access to the information technology, or handle the flow of information, or filter the quantum of information, and thus grab the right opportunity? To overcome this barrier, Nadeem felt that a support group needs to be formed and, from such perspective, the formation of the FDC was a right step forward.

Nadeem started his Hearty Mart Supermarket at Juhapura in the year of 2004. He started expanding his business through franchising in 2007. When he started his franchising venture, he must have felt that his responsibilities would be under stress if he did not develop a second line in command. Luckily, he got Wajir Ali to share his responsibilities. He found leadership qualities and marketing skill in the personal traits of Wajir Ali. Both the traits are very valuable to Nadeem. Nadeem guided and groomed Wajir Ali very closely and thus made him a leader in the organisation. This particular effort of Nadeem has earned the organisation further dividends. For example, Wajir Ali has later groomed three MBA graduates (Deepak, Snehal and Nitin) who have been playing important role in the growth of Hearty Mart group. Since HME looks after procurement and marketing of goods, the information flow between this enterprise and the franchisees is very important. Proper information about prices, discounts, schemes should timely reach the franchisees and, on the other hand, information relating to locally available goods at the franchisees' end does also need to be collected by the enterprise. Thus, quick flow of information through a process of two-way communication helps the whole organisation to take decisions about prices and several other important matters. The MIS (management information system) prepared by the MBA graduates includes regular preparation of sales graph, inventory figure, turnovers etc. This set of information is circulated among the members of top management. Modern education plays an important role in all these activities and monitoring. Wajir felt that if he wants to be a good leader, he needs proper education too. He then enrolled himself at Sikkim Manipal

2. We discuss this in further details later in this chapter.

University and his effort was morally supported by Nadeem. Wajir also followed a short-term course on management at Ahmedabad Management Association (AMA).

Also, filtering and grabbing right information from the flow of galaxy of information needs proper skill which may be earned through professional training. Such need was felt by the top management of Hearty Mart. That is why, Wajir encouraged six of their staff members to enroll in the same short-term course at AMA (the course used to be conducted on Sundays only). The important thing is that the course fees of all the six staff members were borne by Hearty Mart. This means that Hearty Mart is not a narrow-minded organisation; rather, it has a broad vision. Updated information about many pertinent issues of internal market mechanism is not often available from common sources such as internet and newspapers. Wajir has some good connections with several senior executives who are working in FMCG (fast-moving consumer goods) market. He invites some of them—who have experience of more than 10 years—for quick visits at Hearty Mart for lectures or interactions about the market.

Franchisee Development in Villages: Analysis of Different Characteristics of the Individual Franchisees

We now like to compare various aspects of franchisees and examine if any interesting findings could come out in the context of the present discussion. We would also examine the personal characteristics of the franchisees (such as age, education, etc.) in this regard.

Can education of an entrepreneur be regarded as a very important determinant for his success? Perhaps, for a small grocery shop or a pan shop, it may not matter a lot. But, for a supermarket retail outlet, the entrepreneur's education may matter. We have already discussed above this issue, but now we would like to elaborate it further. Since the education system in villages is not at par with that of urban India, we cannot expect that most of the members of the lower and middle income rural families have a chance to go through higher education. Limited education often poses different kinds of problems for village people. Low level of education is often considered as one of the main factors that hinders growth of rural population. Development of entrepreneurship in rural areas is also inhibited by low level of education of the village inhabitants. Table 6.1 suggests that 6 out of 9 franchisees have either 10th standard level education or even lower. Two franchisees (Dholka and Ilol) have achieved 12th standard education. One franchisee (Vadgam) has been found to be graduate. Thus, it is evident from the data that a considerable number of franchisees are trapped into the bounded rationality problem. The franchisees with low level of education may find it difficult to cope up with the fast moving external world that is operating beyond the boundaries of his small village. However, on the other hand, entrepreneurship of a person may also not be found contingent upon one's education. It is often seen that educated people want to opt for salaried employment, rather than self-employment. People from backward section who have limited education may come up as successful entrepreneurs. Hence, other factors such as age, experience, occupational background may also play instrumental role in the success or failure of an entrepreneur. Let us now examine the cases of different franchisees of Hearty Mart in this regard.

Brief Description of the Profiles of Supermarket Franchisees

- The Dholka franchisee (age 29 years) opened the Hearty Mart supermarket store in 2012. As an LIC agent, the Dholka franchisee (Sadiq Ali Momin) was earning ₹20,000 per month before he joined hands with Hearty Mart. According to Table 6.1, the current monthly total income of the franchisee is found to be ₹150,000. This franchisee has done remarkably good since his monthly income has dramatically jumped from ₹35,000 during his initial period with Hearty Mart to ₹150,000 at present (i.e. highest earning among all the franchisees). This means, his spectacular achievement took place in just 3 years. His achievement is also reflected in the number of staff employed in his store. Currently, 12 people are working in his supermarket. In terms of this parameter (i.e. employment), his store stands 2nd among all other franchisees (see Table 6.1). If his supermarket

Table 6.1

Personal and Professional Characteristics of the Franchisor and Franchisees

Sl. No.	Location and Type of Store (E.g. Supermarket or Saral Shop)	Year of Establishment of Hearty Mart Retail Store	Name of Franchisor/ Franchisee	Age of Franchisor/ Franchisee (in Years)	Education of Franchisor/ Franchisee	Work Background Before Joining Hearty Mart	Monthly Income Before Joining Hearty Mart (₹)	Monthly Earning* during Initial Years of Hearty Mart (₹)	Current Monthly Earning* (₹)	No. of Staff Working at The Store
1	Juhapura (supermarket)	2004	Nadeem Jafri (franchisor)	43	MBA	He was employed at an advertising agency	20,000	13,000	75,000	10
2	Dholka (supermarket)	2012	Sadiq Ali Momin (franchisee)	29	12th pass	He was an LIC agent	20,000	35,000	150,000	12
3	Meta (supermarket)	2014	Haidar Ali Ismail (franchisee)	36	10th pass	He was employed at a hotel	15,000	25,000	40,000	4
4	Surat (supermarket)	2011	Jaffar Ali Momin (franchisee)	28	10th fail	He was employed at a petrol-pump	10,000	8,000	26,000	2
5	Vadgam (supermarket)	2013	Asad Khan Pathan (franchisee)	30	B.Com	He was doing business of computer parts and farming	25,000	50,000	75,000	9

6	Chhapi (supermarket)	2014	Hasanbhai Abbas Talsania (franchisee)	35	10th pass	He was unemployed	0	26,000	60,000	13
7	Kanai (saral shop)	2010	Naisam Ali Ahmedabhai Debrotia (franchisee)	50	7th pass	He was engaged in farming	12,000	15,000	25,000	2
8	Pipodar (saral shop)	2012	Abid Hussain Bhatt (franchisee)	41	10th pass	He was owner of a general store	10,000	20,000	35,000	2
9	Ilol (saral shop)	2007	Hasanbhai Abbas Nasir (franchisee)	35	12th pass	He was owner of a general store	3,000	7,000	10,000	2
10	Jethipura** (saral shop)	2010	This franchisee is owned by a village cooperative	-	-	-	-	-	-	2

Note: * Here, earning indicates the amount of money that is drawn by the franchisee, not the profit amount (getting data related to actual profit is difficult). However, from the 'earning' data (which is here used to be a proxy for profit), we can somehow estimate the growth or prosperity of the store.

** Since the Jethipura franchisee is a cooperative, there is no individual level data.

Source: By authors (based on field survey).

was not running well, he could not have employed so many people for his store. Although this person is young (and thus does not have long experience in business) and has limited education (12th pass), he probably does have some finest entrepreneurial qualities. For example, since earlier he has worked as an LIC agent (see Table 6.1), he might have earned experience in public relation as well as personal communication which is an asset for a businessman who has to deal with many customers on regular basis in a retail store. Hence, for growth in business, one's occupational background may sometimes play crucial role.

- Before starting Hearty Mart store, Meta franchisee (age 36 years) was working in a hotel in Mumbai. Neither he was earning handsome money, nor was he able to enjoy the company of his family since he was staying away alone. This shows that due to lack of proper education and skills (see Table 6.1), the opportunity that he can avail in the labour market is limited. But the person wants to grow. For this reason, he quit his earlier job and opened a Hearty Mart franchisee store in his own village. But he is still trapped into bounded rationality problem because neither he could improve his skills, nor could he broaden his exposure. His only satisfaction currently is that he has got the opportunity to stay with his own family in his own village. Of course, both starting a business and expanding a business are contingent upon many variables including stock of capital; but if motivation is grossly suppressed by limited education, skill and exposure, then it is hard to believe that the other factors would sufficiently be able to play a strong supplemental role even if those factors are found favourable to the entrepreneur. Having said so, we cannot overlook the impressive changes in the earnings of the franchisee. The franchisee is currently drawing ₹40,000 per month and this achievement has been witnessed just in one year time (for details, see Table 6.1). Whether or not this franchisee will be able to overcome his limitations in education and experience in the future and grow more is a matter which can only be explored latter. Since the person is young, there is possibility that he would earn experience in the future and lead his business towards faster growth.

- The Surat franchisee (age 28 years) could not pass 10th standard examination. He was employed at a petrol pump before he opened his supermarket under the banner of Hearty Mart. That time he was earning ₹10,000 per month only. When he opened his Hearty Mart supermarket store, his monthly income had even gone down (see Table 6.1). But, currently, he is earning ₹26,000 per month. He started this business in 2011. This means, although he has been able to increase his income more than three times of his initial income in last four years, his present income does not illustrate remarkable growth of his business as compared to the growth of the other 'supermarket' franchisees. Let us keep in mind that his present income may look good as compared to the saral shops, but since he is a supermarket owner, we need to compare his income on the basis of the performance of other supermarket franchisees, not the saral shop franchisees. His slow growth may be attributed to his limited experience (he is too young), low-level of education, etc.
- As we see in Table 6.1, the Vadgam franchisee (age 30 years) is a commerce graduate and he was engaged in both farming and computer-parts related business. But he was not satisfied with his income and occupational profile because he thought that he had much greater potential to grow further. He shared his dissatisfaction with one of his friends and expressed his desire to do some business in retail sector. That friend informed him about the Hearty Mart and subsequently they looked for more information on the internet. He then visited Dholka Hearty Mart outlet and later contacted Nadeem and decided to open his own franchisee outlet. This was the start of his journey with Hearty Mart. As seen in Table 6.1, his growth trajectory

looks impressive after he joined Hearty Mart as a franchisee. For example, he used to earn ₹25,000 per month before he joined Hearty Mart; and his earning has jumped to ₹50,000 per month during his initial days with Hearty Mart while he is currently earning ₹75,000 per month.

- As regards Chappi franchisee (age 35 years), it illustrates quite an impressive growth story in a very short period of time. This man started his Hearty Mart journey only in 2014 before which he was simply unemployed (although sometimes he used to casually help his father who was running a business). He was not much serious about his career. Hearty Mart supermarket is his first and independent business initiative. Immediately after opening the supermarket, he had started earning ₹26,000 per month (see Table 6.1). His currently earning ₹60,000 per month. This indicates huge growth in his business and this looks consistent when we observe that 13 people are currently working in his store. This franchisee has employed highest number of staff among all other franchisees (see Table 6.1). It is astonishing that he has proved himself quite promising franchisee while his educational profile is low. However, he is from business family as his father is engaged in business. He might not have been closely and sincerely associated with his father's business, but he perhaps 'naturally' learned many aspects of business from his father's activities and conduct. Thus, we may infer that family business helps in engendering culture of entrepreneurship in the members of the family.

Brief Description of the Profiles of Saral Shop Franchisees

- The Kanai franchisee (age 50 years) has told us that he did not want to migrate from his own village even when he was not earning sufficient living from his farming activities. He was looking for a decent opportunity which would help him to stay in his own village and earn sufficient money to suffice his family needs. His connection with Nadeem thus has been crucial to find the opportunity of opening a Hearty Mart supermarket store. The educational qualification of the Kanai franchisee owner is even less than 10th standard (see Table 6.1). One thing is to be noted here that since he is 50 years old, he must have acquired enough professional experience in his past life which can be regarded as a treasure for his future journey in the Hearty Mart venture. However, as shown in Table–6.1, his current income is ₹25,000 per month. His Hearty Mart journey started in 2010. From this perspective, his professional achievement in last five years can be termed as moderate. He can achieve more in the future if he can successfully make use of his experience.

- Let us now look at the Pipodar franchisee (age 41 years), who was earlier trying to settle in Hyderabad for a living. However, since this franchisee is highly religious and rooted person, he wanted to remain connected with his own community in Gujarat. He then opened a small general store in his own locality. When he came to know about the Hearty Mart Franchisee opportunity, he wanted to grab it as he was looking for a prosperous life. Like Meta franchisee, he does also have a 10th pass educational qualification with which he was not able to be absorbed in good employment. That is why, as he said, business is the only opportunity which can take him to the path of prosperity. Thus, his motivation for opening this franchisee has come from two factors: 1) his desire to stay in his own village, and 2) his willingness to prosper financially. As shown in Table 6.1, he is currently earning ₹35,000 per month. He was earning ₹10,000 per month before he joined Hearty Mart in 2012. In last three years, the growth of his business looks impressive. Perhaps, his age and corresponding experience, coupled with his entrepreneurial zeal, have contributed to his business growth.
- The Ilol franchisee (age 35 years) was an owner of a general store before he joined hands with Hearty Mart in 2007. He was then earning ₹3,000 per month only (see Table 6.1). His initial earning as a Hearty Mart franchisee was ₹7,000,

whereas he is currently earning ₹10,000 per month. It is surprising that his present growth (as reflected in his present income) does not correspond to his background and experience. He is not new in retail business as he was running a general store earlier and he has gained adequate experience with Hearty Mart too. His educational background is a little better than some other franchisees. But his growth is not found to be satisfactory. This may be because of the fact that he does not have adequate entrepreneurial capabilities or entrepreneurial zeal which is regarded as a primary quality for a person who wants to become an entrepreneur.

- The Jethipura franchise store was started by a local cooperative. There had been no grocery shop in the village before they started it. Villagers had to go to nearby rural town, Jadar, for purchasing the daily necessary items. Thus, the members of the cooperative running the franchisee were motivated to open the store by the opportunity of serving their fellow villagers through selling quality goods at relatively cheap prices (we have described this issue in the previous chapter). They reported that this store offers two opportunities: 1) the villagers do not need to go out of village for grocery shopping; and 2) the cooperative members get connected with the villagers through an income earning activity. So, the Jethipura case represents a unique model in the sense that even when Hearty Mart as an 'organisation' is unable to penetrate a village perhaps because of lack of capital strength of the 'individual' members, a cooperative model emerges as an alternative 'organisation' which promotes itself as a taker of the Hearty Mart Franchisee. So, two organisations join hands of each other in Jethipura, and start a new journey.

Franchisee Development: Bounded Rationality

We have indicated earlier that the lack of awareness of the village franchisees can be depicted as a situation of bounded rationality. They feel that they are living in the safe confines of their own community and thus they do not need to drive for more information and knowledge. This often leads to high transaction cost, especially when people are engaged in some commercial activities with the external world.

The state of Gujarat is growing at a very fast pace. However, the Muslims in the state are unaware of many recent developments due to their lack of education and knowledge. If such a situation continues to persist for a long time then this can lead to organisation failure in an internally linked, but externally delinked, society. Nadeem's intervention through Hearty Mart organisational approach has been able to create a channel between the introverted system and the external environment. The flow of new information through the organisational channel of the Hearty Mart is gradually breaking the rigidity and giving the village community a new shape as well as a new orientation.

- Vadgam franchisee told us that before joining Hearty Mart, he was engaged in farming activities as well as some computer related business. The closed circle which he was living in was not allowing him to explore more opportunity in computer related activity. This problem is rooted in the rigid frame of his community culture. Hearty Mart has been creating a new culture which is open and thus is conducive to create new opportunities.
- When we talked to the franchisees, we realised that they do not have any idea about complex socio-economic realities. To the complex or business environment-related questions they answered monosyllabically. As far as Hearty Mart franchisees are concerned, a paradoxical situation seems to have been appeared. While the external socio-economic situation is very complex, these people are living in a very traditional society with very simple and minimum knowledge, or even sometimes with near misconceptions. This gives us an indication that the franchisees have limits in terms of unpredictable events and are behaving in a set pattern. They seem to be satisfied with the situation that exists in their own domain. It is observed that bounded rationality of the

Chileas is an obstacle to the further growth of Hearty Mart. A new market-based organisational intervention involving Franchisee Development initiated by Hearty Mart Franchiser is conceptualised to slowly eradicate the difference between the external and internal environments.

- Almost similar things are observed in the case of Meta, Kanai and Pipodar franchisees too. The fact that the external conditions are very complex while the Chilea villagers' mental state is very simple may lead to complications when such a franchisee needs to tackle problems or situations outside his own environment. Another interesting matter has been observed in the case of Jethipura franchisee. This store, as said, is a community cooperative which functions based on the inherent trust among the community members living in the village. But who knows that the situation will not change in the future and will not create complications? As economic development proceeds, peoples' perspectives change. Similarly, as the village prospers with time, the simple arrangement under which each village family is currently contributing and benefiting from the cooperative may not continue to remain constant, and the functioning of the cooperative may have to handle complexities. Hearty Mart leaders need to think about this issue for the sustainability of the organisation.

Let us now shed some light on the difference between external and internal environments as per as the Jethipura franchisee is concerned. The Jethipura franchisee owners seem to be feeling that their development will help them attain a bargaining position with the external stakeholders like wholesalers who stay outside the village. If this holds to be true, the opportunistic behaviour of external stakeholders can be tackled. But, what happens if opportunistic behaviour is found to appear in the activities of the internal stakeholders? One may argue that such a situation will not appear due to institutional trust, but, for the sake of the existence and growth of the franchisee in the long run, possible mechanism should be adopted to tackle the opportunistic behaviour of the cooperative members in the future.

Franchisee Development: Religious Bond and Organisation Building through Franchising

Klein (1995) discusses in his article a distinction between franchising arrangements known as 'business format franchisees' (such as McDonalds) and 'product or trade name franchisees'. The former covers "not only the product, service, and trademark, but the entire business format itself—a marketing strategy and plan, operating manuals and standards, quality control, and continuing two-way communication." However, as we see in our study of Hearty Mart as a franchising model, a sharply drawn definition is essentially arbitrary. Therefore, much of the analysis in our study of Hearty Mart as a franchising network follows flexible as well as multidisciplinary approach. Hearty Mart Franchise system represents a model which has grown based on religious-institutional links. As we know, religion often plays important institutional role. Especially, people who belong to the particular cultural and business section within the Islamic religion (e.g. Sufi and business minded Shias/Chileas) have strong fellow feeling and community bonding. The main factor associated with such bond is institutional trust. Hence, the social capital that stems from the trust that is present among the members of the Chilea community is the building block of the formation and proliferation of Hearty Mart franchise model. The institutional trust has played some role in both the spheres—i.e. in the relationship between the franchiser and the franchisee, and in the relationship between the franchisee and the customer. Let us now talk about reputation factor in this regard. Is the reputation of the sect head of the Chilea community important in the growth of Hearty Mart? We think, yes, it is. A conservative member of a religious community feels 'a sense of belonging' while he finds himself under the umbrella of a person he respects as his spiritual guide. He may feel uncomfortable while following orders from someone else. Thus, institutional reputation of Hearty Mart among all the stakeholders is also an important element for the further growth of the model. Let us now for further detail.

- Let us now present our observation regarding institutional trust that we have come across during field survey. As reported by the Dholka franchisee, it has generally two types of buyers: one, those (mainly the local farmers) who visit the store on almost daily basis for purchasing the daily necessary items (whenever they get free from their farming activities); and two, those who visit the store on a particular day of a month for buying grocery items needed for the whole month. The second category consists of mostly the government officials working in public infrastructural development projects under the Gujarat Infrastructural Development Corporation (GIDC) in and around Dholka. These people find Hearty Mart store as one-stop shopping centre as they get all the necessary items under one roof. The Dholka franchisee also reported that the committed Chilea customers staying in the local area have played instrumental role in pulling the government officials towards the Hearty Mart store through verbal publicity. Thus, this shows us how religious institution helps in developing the model of Hearty Mart organisation which is also supported by the publicity (or reputation) created by the local community people.
- As far as the Vadgam Store is concerned, the franchisee owner told us that he is happy in providing new mode of shopping to rural customers. The franchisee owner added that the government is undertaking some infrastructure development projects in the area and this has augmented the level of the income of the local residents. Altogether, there has been a lot of enthusiasm in the minds of the local residents due to two reasons. One, they have been introduced to a supermarket model. Two, their purchasing power went up due to various new economic activities as mentioned above. The second factor seems to be the most important since the local people mostly belong to the LIG (low income group). Another factor is also relevant here according to the

marketing analysis of the franchisee owner itself. Let us explain this. Earlier, the level of sales was relatively much low recently it has increased. Especially, the frequency of the purchases made by the local farmers is very high during 1st day to 5th day and 15th day to 20th day of every month. Such increase in frequency is caused by the fact that banks have given Kissan Credit Card to farmers who own land. This credit facility has given the farmers an extra opportunity to purchase items in large quantities. Due to credit cards, farmers have started cattle rearing for dairy business to earn extra income. As we know, there is correlation between increase in one's income and change in lifestyle from traditional to urban/modern trends. Hence, the introduction of modern retail format in Vadgam has been very timely since the income levels of the local people have started going up. Their concept of shopping has recently changed from basic need-based purchase to some higher level. The 'higher level' includes basic need-based purchase plus lifestyle-based purchase which is immensely influenced by the modern media such as television, films, internet, smartphone etc.

This franchisee reported that his range of market in terms of geographical area covers wide peripheries as they deliver goods at villages which are 22 km away from their store, if they receive calls for home delivery. It is amazing that the store has not yet gone through any kinds of publicity activities, but still it has been receiving telephonic orders for home delivery from very far villages (home delivery is provided at free of cost). It shows the power of influence of modern lifestyle (supermarket shopping, home-delivery service, etc.) on village households.

- The Meta store owner told us that the customers do not only come to his store to purchase items for their daily consumption needs, but also to purchase items for their social or occasional functions such as marriage, religious get together etc. For such type of functions, the store receives bulk orders which it delivers at very reasonable prices. In this regard, the price factor helps him to attract greater number of customers.

- As far as Pipodar store is concerned, it also caters to the needs of the middle and LIG people in the village. However, high income group people do not show much interest in this store because they prefer to go to Himmantnagar—which is a bigger town—for purchasing certain items such as foodgrains, edible oil, etc. in bulk quantity for annual consumption. To attract this group, this franchise owner has been gradually going through changes in strategies. For several products, he is upgrading his sales strategy from single brand of an item to multiple brands of the same. For example, earlier he used to sell coconut oil of Parachute brand, but he has now started offering the brands such as Hair and Care too. Similarly, he is now selling Garnier Hair Colour along with Godrej Hair Dye. These new additions are being made with an objective of making his store somewhat comparable with the urban stores, on the one hand, and more competitive than the other local stores, on the other. Overall, we can consider the Hearty Mart store as an 'intermediary store' which is somewhat better than the other local stores but, at the same time, is not able to compete fully with the urban stores.
- Let us now look at the Kanai store. Most of the customers of this store belongs to the middle class and the LIG. The store owner is mainly interested to capture the people of these two classes because they are the majority in the area. In the initial months, as he said, he kept a close watch on customers' choices. This means, he conducted an informal survey on his customers and from the survey he learnt that he would need to stock all those types of commodities which are affordable by consumers of middle and LIGs. He said that he had been advised by the FDC to closely study his customers' choices. This advice has helped him a lot. An important point that he shared with us is that since his villagers are happy with the Hearty Mart sales approaches,

he is also enjoying working with the Hearty Mart franchiser. Thus, we see that an 'institutional trust' has been developed among the parties involved. Through the religious root, Hearty Mart has been able to create a 'new institution' which combines both religious organisation and business organisation. Although the Kanai franchisee owner is from the Muslim community, he has good communication with other local community people too. That is why he does good business during both the festivals—Eid and Diwali.

Degree of Autonomy in Hearty Mart Model

All the franchisees in Hearty Mart enjoy adequate independence and autonomy as far as certain decision-making processes are concerned. Although centralised intervention is evident in the model, decentralised bodies have been given enough autonomy to make decisions at their own level. Let us take a look into this through the following observations.

- How an organisation deals with both centralisation and flexibility (or, maintaining a balance between these two) with regard to their functioning is an interesting matter. But it is not the case that there is no supervision at all. Supervision is undertaken periodically by the franchiser. Monthly visit by Nadeem is paid to each and every franchisee. Further, the FDC meetings are organised in every month.
- During interviews, we came to know that the franchisee such as Pipodar does not take advice frequently from the franchiser. His arguments are very unique. He said that the franchiser is located in the city whereas his store is located in a village. According to him, the mentalities of city customers and village customers differ from each other. Thus, since the conditions are different, their marketing strategies and several other things may not be similar. In such case, informal contract with the franchiser helps both of them to maintain a distinct but cordial business relationship. The conflict will not arise since the franchisee has not been asked to follow any strict terms and conditions.

- In a community with good and robust religious network, there may be almost complete sharing of information whatever available. As far as the business information or commercial information is concerned, Hearty Mart has been facilitating flow of information through the channel of FDC and several other informal means. This gives us an example of the fact that if price does not communicate important market related information (because the information pertaining to fluctuations in prices may not always reach some market agents staying in remote areas); the situation can be dealt with by means of organisational coordination. This means, information relating to fluctuations in prices, new discounts, new offers, etc. can be circulated through internal institutional channel. Thus, the centralised information gathering process and subsequent circulation of information to the decentralised units help grow this business.
- The store at Meta likes to purchase goods from the local producers at village. For example, they procure 'Green Bungalow Tea' from a local manufacturer. This gives us the example of how flexible the organisational system is. Even he is thinking to opt for more local purchases in the future, if he gets good quality products. Thus, informal contracts often help decentralised small organisation to grow in their own way as they find suitable.
- The Kanai store is another example. It does not procure goods from the parent body rather it prefers to purchase items from its nearby town, Himmatnagar, because it is convenient and cost effective for him.

Some Further Observations

An organisation is often shaped and influenced by the local (or regional), social, political and other related milieu. In return, the organisation also responds to its milieu in the similar way. For instance, Vadgam customer-base includes both farmers and non-farmers. It is often imperative for the store owner to offer products to such village level customers at discounted rates. Keeping this in view, Vadgam franchisee makes its own strategies to attract the local customers. While doing so, the seasonal and festival issues are also taken into account.

- Dholka Franchisee has good aptitude towards inventory management. He is good in predicting the customer demand during the special occasions like Ramadan, Diwali, Janmashtami, etc. He gave us an example. Since he has good knowledge about the sale and stocks of dry fruits during Ramdan festival last year, the stock that is required for this year is estimated by him very well. That is what we came to know from him and his staff members. He told us that he keeps himself updated about the variations in demands for different goods in different seasons. For example, he knows very well about how much quantity of maida or sugar has to be procured during the festival of Janmashtami. Such inventory management skill helps him in his financial management part too.
- Let us now discuss some of the problems faced by the Vadgam franchisee and how he is responding to them. He was talking to us about building of organisation through cooperation. Vadgam franchisee owner says that conflicts may arise in any organisation, but he believes in working with harmony. He values long-term cooperation, rather than stretching temporary conflicts. He explains that if he has difference of opinion with a dealer or distributor, he would first try to solve the problem amicably. In case a distributor delays the supply then, as he says, he would humbly alert him of the fact. Initially, he used to get the supply from the Hearty Mart's Ahmedabad-based store. He was not much aware of the demand and he used to face repeatedly the problem of stock due to his poor inventory management caused by his conservative approach. He was conservative because he did not want to stock more than the quantity demanded by the customers in a specific period of time. For this conservative approach, stocks often used to be exhausted before the products were supplied by the Hearty Mart Ahmedabad

store. On the other hand, the Hearty Mart Ahmedabad store does not supply goods very frequently (they only supply products twice a month). Even if they want to supply, it may not be cost effective since quantity demanded by the franchisee is really small. Vadgam franchisee told us that this problem was not predicted before joining hands with Hearty Mart. Overall, his inability to satisfy the customer demand (in several occasions) owing to shortage of stock has negatively impacted his business. Sometimes he opted for a solution to this problem by having interim stocks or products of companies such as ITC.

- Coordination between the franchisee and the franchiser is an important aspect of a franchisee model which is grossly contingent upon informal contracts. There is good coordination between the franchiser and most of the franchisees within Hearty Mart. Let us give an example of such coordination vis-à-vis policy dilemma. Initially, Vadgam franchisee used to sell commodities to some of his customers on credit of maximum 15 days. Rural customers generally want to purchase items on credit. Although the rural retailers can gain popularity if they allow credit to their customers, sometimes it is difficult for the retailers to chase the recovery. Especially, it is difficult for a modern supermarket-type retailer. Since the Juhapura-based franchiser has a good coordination with his franchisees, the franchiser came to know about the credit policy of the Vadgam franchisee. The franchiser suggested the franchisee not to allow credit to the customers on random basis and in huge amount. The Vadgam franchisee told us that they are thinking about the pros and cons of the non-credit policy. But they have not finally decided anything about it.
- Let us now look at another interesting aspect. How can one retailer gain trust of his customers? This can be done in several ways. One, the retailer may offer good quality products, which can earn him some reputation as well as trust in the market. Two, personal rapport with the

customers in the rural areas is also an important factor. An organisational framework often helps in building the brand and thus reputation and trust as well. The Hearty Mart franchiser has been able to successfully pass on this message to their franchisees. The franchisees are also following the guidance. The nature of rural customer is very different from that of urban customers. The Hearty Mart franchisees, as we have been told, are maintaining good rapport with their customers through personal interaction.

Flexibility in Product Range

There is no fixed guideline about the product range in the Hearty Mart organisation. The franchisees have been given freedom to sell products according to the local needs. For example, Vadgam franchisee sells, among many other items, baby care products and a range of plastic crockery sets which were never sold in its locality before Hearty Mart started. However, due to emerging markets of innovative products and products of new design, the village franchisees are also facing competition. For example, a new store has come up near the Vadgam franchisee with plastic products only. Since competition is considered to be healthy for a market to grow, Vadgam franchisee owner told us that he is taking it positively and he wants to further upgrade his store in the near future. But, as far as the baby care products are concerned, there is still not a single store in the entire Vadgam area, which sells such type of products. Thus, Vadgam franchisee has huge advantage in this specific product market, unless another store comes up in the area. The franchisees keep doing experiments with the interior arrangements which the local general stores never came up with because they did not feel to do so. Let us give an example of an innovative idea of Vadgam franchisee. In the last summer, they started selling sunglasses for the local customers. This is such a product which no general store has ever thought of selling.

As far as price is concerned, the Hearty Mart franchisee goods are highly competitive because of several reasons. Let us give an example. In general, if the retailer allows some company or distributor to launch any publicity scheme or advertisement in favour of the company or the distributor, then the retailer gets some incentives. Some of the franchisee owners convert such incentives as discount on the prices of the commodities. Hence, finally such incentives are passed on to the customers in the form of discounted price. The other general stores, as we have been told, generally do not follow such policy. This gives Hearty Mart franchisee a competitive advantage over others.

Some Strategies

Recently, the FDC has suggested the franchisees to stock some products 'well in advance' in larger quantities before certain festivals. They found that demand for sugar, maida (flour), edible oil, etc. goes up during some popular festivals. All the franchisees have followed the suggestions of the FDC and thus benefitted because they earned some non-seasonal (non-festival) discounts on bulk purchase. This helps them to sell some products at less than market price during festivals. This has additional benefits in the sense that when a customer comes to purchase any non-discounted product/s, s/he is attracted to the additional discounted product/s as well. Moreover, many personal care products are now sold at Hearty Mart stores, which were earlier not available in the village areas. This has changed the consumer behaviour in some way. For example, earlier local people used such products occasionally only. Another important finding is that Hearty Mart Vadgam franchisee is closely connected to the people. For example, the store contributes to the functions such as Muharram and Navratri. The franchisee contributes to organising of Garba and thus they have been maintaining good public relation with the local communities.

However, as far as public relation is concerned, the Dholka franchisee has a different strategy. They want to give an emotional touch to their communication while dealing with local customers. When a customer visits their store, s/he is addressed or greeted with her/his first name and, as the franchisee said, this helps customer to feel honoured.

This franchisee has introduced many branded items in the store. For example, ashirwad ata is not sold anywhere in entire Dholka, except for this franchisee. Hearty Mart franchisee store is the only seller which sells it and it is now one of the most demanded items. This franchisee attracts customers by offering discount on (edible) oil prices because Dholka market is highly influenced by oil market as well as oil prices. Once a customer visits the store for discounted oil, s/he often purchases other commodities as well. The franchisee owner told us that, due to such discount, his current year's sale has increased by 30 per cent compared to the last year's sale which, in turn, has had a positive impact on the profit.

Conclusion

In this chapter, our aim was to understand the Hearty Mart franchising supermarket model in the light of the empirical observations. We have conducted interviews with the franchiser and the franchisees. The qualitative data analysis has been presented in this chapter. In the light of the organisational economics, we have discussed elaborately the important issues such as coordination, institutional trust, reputation, property rights, bounded rationality conditions, contracts, informal relation, and inventory management, among others. The Hearty Mart franchiser is located in the city of Ahmedabad whereas the franchisees are located in villages. This is a unique type of 'supermarket franchising model' which has been developed based on institutional trust, solidarity and informal relation. This has facilitated a new development through which rural customers are getting an exposure of urban shopping style in the Hearty Mart supermarket outlets located in their own areas.

7

Hearty Mart from the Lenses of the Customers

Introduction

As already discussed, Hearty Mart is a community-oriented franchising network that has retail outlets in several villages of Gujarat. The organisation consists of a group of franchisers on the one hand and a number of franchisees on the other. The details of the organisation itself and its aspects of social entrepreneurship have been discussed in detail in the previous chapters. The customers' behaviour is an important aspect of this study, which has not been discussed yet. It is imperative to examine the determinants of customers' behaviour to learn the growth trajectory of the Hearty Mart retailing in villages. In this task, we would like to divide the Hearty Mart retail units into two categories—supermarket and saral shop. Supermarkets are larger in size than saral shops and the latter is located in very remote places as compared to the former. For supermarkets, 300 sample customers have been interviewed, whereas for saral shops, 80 customers have been interviewed. The sample customers have been invited to take part in the research at the door of the various retail outlets on particular dates while the customers were getting out of the stores after their shopping. Hence, we have followed the convenience sampling procedure (non-probability sampling technique). The data have been collected from 6 supermarket locations (50 samples from each location) and from 4 saral shop locations (20 samples from each location). For details, see Appendix A-7.1. Let us now analyse the data in the following section.

Note that, as indicated above, the empirical analysis in this chapter comprises two sets of data: 1) Hearty Mart supermarket data and 2) Hearty Mart saral shop data. In most of the sections, these two types of data will be presented in combined tables. That is, separate columns will be used for supermarkets and saral shops in one table; and, in addition, the total of the supermarket and saral shop will be shown in a separate column in the same table. However, our analysis of the tables will attempt to capture the issues of supermarket and saral shop separately in detail, and their 'total' will be considered self-explanatory.

Customer's Visits (Number of Days in a Month) at Hearty Mart Stores

According to Table 7.1, maximum number of customers are found to be visiting Hearty Mart supermarket for 1–5 days in a month. Similar is the case for Hearty Mart saral shops. This indicates that majority of the customers—in both supermarket and saral shop—perhaps prefer to do their grocery shopping in a few visits in a month. As regards supermarket, Table 7.1 shows that as the number of visits in a month goes up, the proportion of customers more or less goes down. We find slightly different picture in the case of saral shops. As far as the number of visits is concerned, 10 per cent of customers have been found to have visited the saral shops for 25–30 days in a month. This indicates that saral shops are located in the places where

Table 7.1

Number of Days the Respondent Visits the Store in a Month

No. of Days the Respondent Visits the Store in a Month	*Supermarket*		*Saral Shop*		*Total*	
	No. of Customer	*Per cent*	*No. of Customer*	*Per cent*	*No. of Customer*	*Per cent*
1 to 5	231	77.00	50	62.50	281	73.90
6 to 10	46	15.33	14	17.50	60	15.8
11 to 15	17	5.67	3	3.75	20	5.2
16 to 20	2	0.67	2	2.50	4	1.1
21 to 25	0	0.00	3	3.75	3	0.8
26 to 30	4	1.33	8	10.00	12	3.2
All	300	100.00	80	100.00	380	100.00

at least some customers are very much dependent on saral shops for their grocery shopping on almost daily basis. Perhaps, the number of grocery shops are very limited in those areas and simultaneously, some customers prefer to do grocery shopping in very small quantity at every visit as per their daily needs (for which they are to visit saral shops for 26–30 days in a month).

Income Pattern of the Customers

It is evident from the supermarket data in Table 7.2 that the LIG (low income group) (₹1000–₹10,000 as monthly income) and the low-MIG (middle income group) (₹10,001–₹20,000 as monthly income) jointly constitute the largest proportion (84.7%) of the total number of the customers. The relatively high income group constitutes a small proportion of the total number of customers. This finding is further substantiated by the supplementary observations. For example, let us look at the supermarket data in Table 7.3 which shows that the majority (76%) of the customers belong to LIG (bottom of pyramid) in terms of the per capita monthly family income (₹0–₹3,000). The customers that belong to the range of monthly per capita family income of ₹3,001–₹5,000 account for 18.7 per cent. More or less similar observations are found in the case of saral shops too. One of the objectives of the Hearty Mart organisation is to provide the

Table 7.2

Distribution of Customers According to Income Range of the Family

Income Range of the Family (in ₹ per month)	*Supermarket*		*Saral shop*		*Total*	
	No. of Customer	*Per cent*	*No. of Customer*	*Per cent*	*No. of Customer*	*Per cent*
₹1000 to 10,000	129	43	43	53.75	172	45.26
₹10,001 to 20,000	125	41.7	29	36.25	154	40.53
₹20,001 to 30,000	41	13.7	4	5	45	11.84
₹30,001 to 40,000	2	0.7	2	2.5	4	1.05
₹40,001 to 50,000	2	0.7	1	1.25	3	0.79
Above ₹50,000	1	0.3	1	1.25	2	0.53
All	300	100	80	100	380	100.00

services of organised retailing to the low-income people in villages of Gujarat. The data shows that Hearty Mart has more or less been able to fulfil its objective.

Table 7.3

Composition of Customers in Terms of Per Capita Income of the Family

Income per-capita per Month	*Supermarket*		*Saral Shop*		*Total*	
	No. of Customer	*Per cent*	*No. of Customer*	*Per cent*	*No. of Customer*	*Per cent*
₹0–₹3,000	228	76	66	82.5	294	77.37
₹3,001–₹5,000	56	18.7	7	8.75	63	16.58
₹5001–₹10,000	15	5	7	8.75	22	5.79
Above ₹10,001	1	0.3	0	0	1	0.26
All	300	100	80	100	380	100.00

Accessibility to Non-Hearty Mart Stores

Table 7.4 shows that 93 per cent of the supermarket customers said that there is other store near their home and more than 45 per cent of the total number of the supermarket customers said that they visited stores other than Hearty Mart in the last one month to purchase some household items. This indicates that a considerable proportion of the total number of supermarket customers do visit both Hearty Mart supermarket stores and other stores. This means, there is competition between Hearty Mart supermarket stores and other stores in the places where Hearty Mart supermarket stores are located. The positive indication of the growth of the Hearty Mart stores is observed when we see that more than 47 per cent of the total number of customers did not visit other stores in the last one month. As far as the saral shops are concerned, more than 33 per cent of the customers said that there are no other stores near their home except the Hearty Mart saral shops. So, unlike the Hearty Mart supermarket customers, a moderately considerable proportion of saral shop customers are dependent on Hearty Mart saral shops. Again, this proves that by and large Hearty Mart has fulfilled a social objective by setting up retail stores at remote areas. Interestingly, in the case of saral shops, more than 43 per cent of the total number of customers, who have access to non-Hearty Mart stores near their house, are found to have not visited them in the last one month. This means that they prefer Hearty Mart stores to other stores.

Table 7.4

Respondent's Accessibility to Non-Hearty Mart Stores vis-à-vis Hearty Mart Stores

Are There Any Other Stores or Shops Nearby Your Home or in Village?	*Supermarket*		*Saral Shop*		*Total*	
	No. of Customer	*Per cent*	*No. of Customer*	*Per cent*	*No. of Customer*	*Per cent*
Yes	279	93	53	66.25	332	87.37
• Those who visited the other stores in last one month	136	45.33	18	22.5	154	40.53
• Those who didn't visit the other stores in last one month	143	47.67	35	43.75	178	46.84
No	21	7	27	33.75	48	12.63
Total	300	100	80	100	380	100

Frequency of Visit to Non-Hearty Mart Store

The growth of Hearty Mart in terms of customer's visit is further supported when we look at Table 7.5 which illustrates that 77 per cent of the supermarket customers have reduced their visit to other stores after they have started visiting Hearty Mart supermarket stores. More interesting picture is observed in the case of Hearty Mart saral shops. We see that more than 91 per cent of the customers have reduced visiting other retail stores after they started visiting Hearty Mart saral shops. One of the reasons is that some saral shops have been set up in remote areas where there was no retail store prior to Hearty Mart has opened up their stores. For example, earlier, the residents of Jethipura village used to go to the nearest town, Jadar, for their daily shopping, which is quite a few kilometers away from their village. Currently, the Hearty Mart retail store is the obvious choice of the villagers of Jethipura. That is why the data reflects overwhelming bias in favour of Hearty Mart saral shops.

Table 7.5

Visit to Hearty Mart Supermarket vis-à-vis Other Stores

Have You Reduced Your Visit to Other Retail Stores after You Started Visiting Hearty Mart	*Supermarket*		*Saral shop*		*Total*	
	No. of Customer	*Per cent*	*No. of Customer*	*Per cent*	*No. of Customer*	*Per cent*
Yes	231	77	73	91.25	304	80
No	69	23	7	8.75	76	20
Total	300	100	80	100	380	100

Discounts

According to Table 7.6, the customers that have reported that some discount is available at Hearty Mart supermarket stores account for 87 per cent, out of which more than 78 per cent of the total number of supermarket customers said that the discount given in the Hearty Mart store is 'generally' greater than that of other stores. Hence, this could be identified as one of the determining factors as to why a large proportion of customers have been reducing their visits to other stores.

As Table 7.6 depicts, 13 per cent of the Hearty Mart supermarket customers said that they do not receive any discount from Hearty Mart stores. Moreover, more than 8 per cent of the supermarket customers said that the discounts that they get from the Hearty Mart supermarket stores are less than that of other stores. Hence, in total, more than 21 per cent of the Hearty Mart supermarket customers gave us contradictory views as compared to the responses we received from more than 78 per cent of supermarket customers (as already mentioned above). Thus, the discount policy and its dissemination need to be reviewed by the Hearty Mart group, keeping in view the fact that a certain section of its customers are not benefitting (either not benefitting adequately, or not benefitting at all) from its discount policy. Since a good majority of the customers said that they are getting discounts, there is a reason to believe that discounts drew attention of a considerable section of the local people. But, as far as scalability is concerned (as mentioned in chapter 5 which discusses social entrepreneurship), the Hearty Mart group needs to analyse the negative response given by more than 21 per cent of the Hearty Mart supermarket customers. If the proper dissemination of the discounts given is not taking place, then the lacuna in this regard should be remedied for further growth of the stores.

However, since more than 78 per cent of the Hearty Mart supermarket customers have reported that they are getting adequate discounts, this indicates that Hearty Mart stores fulfil one of the criteria of social enterprise. The fact that we have stated in chapter 5 regarding discounts (i.e. the views of the franchisee owners) is now substantiated by the responses of customers. According to Nadeem Jafri, Hearty Mart has not been established and promoted to make profits only. While profit is an important aspect of a commercial activity, the social cause gets equal priority when the commercial activity operates within the framework of social enterprise. One of the objectives of Hearty Mart is to cater to certain specific needs of the rural residents (a section of which is poor): in this perspective, Hearty Mart has been grossly able to achieve its objective when a large proportion of customers express their satisfaction in getting discounts that are higher than that offered by the other stores.

In continuation of the above discussion, let us take a look at the saral shop data in Table 7.6 which illustrates the views of customers regarding the saral shops. More than 71 per cent of saral shop customers say that they get discounts on their purchases at Hearty Mart saral shop stores and all of them agree that the discounts they receive are 'generally' higher than that of other stores. However, more than 28 per cent of saral shop customers report that they receive no discounts from the saral shops. The Hearty Mart group needs to critically review this finding.

Table 7.6

Discount at Hearty Mart

Do You Get Discount on Your Purchases at the Hearty Mart	*Supermarket*		*Saral Shop*		*Total*	
	No. of Customer	*Per cent*	*No. of Customer*	*Per cent*	*No. of Customer*	*Per cent*
Yes	261	87	57	71.25	318	83.68
• The discount is greater than that of other stores	236	78.66	57	71.25	293	77
• The discount is less than that of other stores	25	8.33	0	0	25	7
No	39	13	23	28.75	62	16.32
Total	300	100	80	100	380	100.00

Home Delivery Services

Hearty Mart provides home delivery service for their customers and illustration of this has been given in Table 7.7a. Of the total number of supermarket customers, more than 65 per cent customers said that they are aware of the home delivery service provided by the Hearty Mart supermarket stores. However, little more than 27 per cent of supermarket customers have made use of the home delivery service so far. As many as 37.66 per cent of supermarket customers have not yet used this service. Let us now take a look at the reasons for why some supermarket customers used home delivery service and some others did not. According to Table 7.7b, the majority (69.88%) of the users of the Hearty Mart supermarket home delivery service say that they avail this service when they buy goods in bulk quantity. About 20 per cent of the users said that they avail this service in order to save their time. More than 8 per cent of the other users said that they avail this service during the seasonal purchase (e.g. festival time). Let us look at Table 7.7c for further illustration. The Hearty Mart supermarket customers who know about this service but have not yet used this (i.e. 113 supermarket customers) reported the following reasons for not using so: 1) the respondent did not purchase goods in bulk (61.06%), 2) the store is located very close to the respondent's house (23.01%), and 3) the respondent preferred to visit the store in person and do the shopping on his/her own (15.93%).

Table 7.7a

Home Delivery Service

Do you know that Home Delivery Service is Provided by this store?	*Supermarket*		*Saral Shop*		*Total*	
	No. of Customer	*Per cent*	*No. of Customer*	*Per cent*	*No. of Customer*	*Per cent*
Yes, I know about their home delivery service	196	65.33	66	82.5	262	69
• I use home delivery service	83	27.66	1	1.25	84	22
• I do not use home delivery service	113	37.66	65	81.25	178	47
I do not know about their home delivery service	104	34.66	14	17.5	118	31
Total	300	100	80	100	380	100

Table 7.7b

Why Do You Use Home Delivery Service (Supermarket Customers)?

Why Do You Use Home Delivery Service?	*No. of Customer*	*Per cent*
When I buy goods in bulk quantity (i.e. heavy weight)	58	69.88
To save my time	16	19.28
In special need (e.g. seasonal purchase/festival time)	7	8.43
It is generally convenient	2	2.41
Total	83	100

Table 7.7c

Why Don't You Use Home Delivery Service (Supermarket Customers)?

Why Don't You Use Home Delivery Service?	*No. of Customer*	*Per cent*
The store is near to my home	26	23.01
I do not buy many items at a time or in bulk	69	61.06
I prefer to visit the store and do the shopping	18	15.93
Total	113	100

As far as saral shops are concerned (see Table 7.7), a majority (82.5%) of the respondents said that they know about the home delivery services but they have hardly used the service (as 81.25% of the total number of saral shop customers said that they have not used the service). As many as 17.5 per cent saral shop customers said that they do not know about this service. As we said earlier, the saral shops are located in remote villages where people prefer to buy goods in small quantities as and when needed. This might be the reason for their much reluctance towards the home delivery service.

Purchasing Pattern

We asked the customers a question as to what they 'normally' purchase from the Hearty Mart stores. Evidence suggests that most of the supermarket customers (87.33%) visit Heart Mart supermarket stores for purchasing the grocery items (Table 7.8). Cosmetics/toiletries account for a little more than 10 per cent of the supermarket customers. Only 2.33 per cent supermarket customers visit the stores for miscellaneous items such as deodorants, fruit juice, chocolates, snacks, etc. The composition suggests that grocery items are at the centre of attraction for the Hearty Mart supermarket customers. As we have seen in Table 7.2 and Table 7.3, Hearty Mart stores are mostly visited by the LIG and the low-MIG. This corresponds with the finding given in Table 7.8, when we see that a

Table 7.8

Normally What Do You Buy from Hearty Mart

What Do You 'normally' buy from the Hearty Mart?	*Supermarket*		*Saral shop*		*Total*	
	No. of Customer	*Per cent*	*No. of Customer*	*Per cent*	*No. of Customer*	*Per cent*
Grocery	262	87.33	75	93.75	337	88.68
Cosmetics/toiletries	31	10.33	5	6.25	36	9.47
Other items (such as deodorant/juice/chocolate/cold drink/chips/biscuit/milkshake/butter milk/underwear etc.)	7	2.33	0	0	7	1.84
Total	300	100	80	100	380	100

good majority of the customers 'normally' visit Hearty Mart stores for buying grocery items. Although 76 per cent of the customers have a per capita monthly income of ₹3,000 which is considered to be moderately low, the scopes for selling other interesting items need to be explored by the Hearty Mart group for further prosperity of their stores. As far as the saral shops are concerned, a huge majority (93.75%) of the customers visit the stores for grocery shopping. This goes in line with our expectation.

Comparison of Services between Hearty Mart Stores and Other Stores

Let us now look at Table 7.9 to examine the perception of the customers about the services provided by the Hearty Mart supermarket stores as compared to the other stores. As far as the services provided by the Hearty Mart supermarket stores are concerned, majority (51.33%) of the respondents could not give us specific answer and thus simply replied 'not sure'. Although 39.33 per cent of the respondents said that they received better services from the Hearty Mart supermarket stores when compared to other stores (while only 9.33% said that they received services poor than other stores), the 'not sure' category seems to appear as a concern for the Hearty Mart group. The Hearty Mart organisation needs to take a challenge to convert the customers' answer from 'not sure' to 'better'. Since the majority, i.e. 51.33 per cent of the respondents, opted for the answer 'not sure', this may have indirectly indicated that these customers want the services provided by the Hearty Mart supermarket stores to be further improved. A social enterprise not only needs to take care of the 'basic purposes' (supplying goods at the remote places) of the people concerned, it should also supplement the core objective with quality services (better services). In the case of saral shops, the customers' responses mostly went in favour of the Hearty Mart stores (not shown in Table 7.9, since almost all respondents preferred Hearty Mart services) since the other stores are located in distant places. Prior to the Hearty Mart saral shops were set-up in their villages, there were virtually no grocery shop at all. So, the villagers are happy with the Hearty Mart stores.

Table 7.9

Comparison of Services between Hearty Mart Supermarkets and Other Stores

In General, What is Your Perception About the Services Provided by the Hearty Mart Stores as Compared to Other Stores?	*No. of Customer*	*Per cent*
Better	118	39.33
Poor	28	9.33
Not Sure	154	51.33
Total	300	100

Quality of Products at Hearty Mart

As far as social enterprise is concerned, the quality of goods is an important aspect of it. We asked the sample customers a question related to their perception about the quality of products available at Hearty Mart stores as compared to other stores that they have visited in their locality (see Table 7.10). More than 87 per cent of the supermarket customers have replied that in general, they have found Hearty Mart supermarket products to be superior to that of other stores. More or less similar findings are observed in the case of Hearty Mart saral shops as well (see Table 7.10).

Table 7.10

Quality of Products at Hearty Mart

How do You Compare Quality of Hearty Mart Products with that of Other Stores?	*Supermarket*		*Saral Shop*		*Total*	
	Superior	*Inferior*	*Superior*	*Inferior*	*Superior*	*Inferior*
No. of Customers (and ercentage)	262 (87.33)	38 (12.66)	75 (93.75)	5 (6.25)	337 (88.68)	43 (11.32)

Note: Figures in bracket indicate the percentages relative to the total.

Accessibility

As far as the Hearty Mart supermarkets are concerned, about 50 per cent of their customers are from nearby areas (i.e. Hearty Mart stores are located close to their home) (see Table 7.11). More than 33 per cent customers are from far places (i.e. between 1 km and 2 kms). Interestingly, about 17 per cent of the total number of customers are from very far places. In the case of saral shops, more than 67 per cent of the total number of customers are from nearby places (see Table 7.11). Hence, the proportions of customers that visit saral shops from far and very far places are less than that of supermarkets. This indicates that the Hearty Mart supermarkets are more successful in drawing the attention of customers residing at relatively distant places than the saral shops are.

Table 7.11

How Much Time Does it Take to Reach the Supermarket from Your Home?

How Much Time Does it Take to Reach the Supermarket from Your Home?	*Supermarket*		*Saral Shop*		*Total*	
	No. of Customer	*Per cent*	*No. of Customer*	*Per cent*	*No. of Customer*	*Per cent*
Close to my place (<1 km)	135	49.74	54	67.5	189	49.74
Far (between 1 km and 2 kms)	108	33.42	19	23.75	127	33.42
Very far (>2 kms)	57	16.84	7	8.75	64	16.84
Total	300	100	80	100	380	100

Stock Availability

How efficient are the Hearty Mart managers in the case of inventory management? Let us try to know the views of the customers about this. As many as 40 per cent of the supermarket customers reported that they had come across the problem of shortage of items or out-of-stock problem in the stores (see Table 7.12). However, 60 per cent of the supermarket customers did not come across such problems. We asked a further question to those supermarket customers who found out-of-stock problem in supermarket stores. The question is: do you visit other stores, or do you wait for new stocks to arrive? A section of the supermarket customers, i.e. 23.66 per cent of the supermarket customers, reported that they visit other stores when the required item is not available at the Hearty Mart supermarket stores (Table 7.12). To retain this section, the Hearty Mart group needs to sit together and think about better inventory management. As regards saral shops, more than 77 per cent of the total number of customers said that they did not face the problem of shortage of items in the stores (see Table 7.12). Although more than 22 per cent of the total number of customers have faced the out-of-stock problem, the proportion of the customers who have moved to other stores to find their choice is not significantly high (it accounts for 6.25%). Perhaps, this is because of the fact that they do not have any other choice since there are very limited number of grocery shops near their villages. However, to increase the scalability of Hearty Mart organisation, every customer should be regarded as important part of it, and, thus, Hearty Mart should act accordingly.

Table 7.12

Responses in Case of Shortages

Do You Sometime Face Shortage of Items, or out-of-Stock Problem?	*Supermarket*		*Saral shop*		*Total*	
	No. of Customer	*Per cent*	*No. of Customer*	*Per cent*	*No. of Customer*	*Per cent*
Yes	120	40	18	22.5	138	36.32
• If yes, you visit other stores	71	23.66	5	6.25	76	20.00
• If yes, you wait for new stocks to arrive	49	16.33	13	16.25	62	16.32
No	180	60.00	62	77.50	242	63.68
Total	300	100	80	100	380	100.00

Indentifying the Product in the Store

As far as the modern supermarket concept is concerned, customers are given autonomy to enter into the store and directly reach the items displayed for sale. And the customers can themselves pick-up the products that they want to purchase. If the display is not properly arranged, the customer may not easily reach the proper shelf and identify the required product he is looking for. Since saral shops are small in size and do not follow the supermarket format, we have collected data from the supermarket customers only. And, we found that more than 93 per cent of the customers could easily identify the required product in the store (see Table 7.13).

Table 7.13

Can the Customer Easily Identify the Required Product in the Hearty Mart Supermarket Store?

Is it Easy to Identify Required Products in the Hearty Mart Supermarket Store You Visited?	*No. of Customer*	*Per cent*
Yes, it is easy to identify	281	93.67
• same facility also available in other stores in the locality	142	47.33
• similar facility is not available in other stores in the locality	139	46.33
No, it is not easy to identify	19	6.33
Total	300	100.00

Range of Brands

The supermarket stores, in general, keep varieties of brands of a particular product in their retail outlets in order to help customers to choose his desired one/s according to his preference in terms of price, quality, quantity, etc. Relating to this, we asked a question to the customers of Hearty Mart supermarkets. Table 7.14 suggests that most of the customers (93%) are satisfied with the range of brands available in Hearty Mart supermarkets.

Table 7.14

Range of Brands Available at Hearty Mart Supermarket Store

Do You Get Better Range of Brands as Compared to Other Stores?	*No. of Customer*	*Per cent*
Yes	279	93.00
No	21	7.00
Total	300	100.00

Billing Experience

One of the objectives of Hearty Mart supermarket is to provide modern facility to the village customers. The rural traditional retail stores either give their customers no bill (or receipt) at all, or they do follow manual billing system. Hearty Mart has introduced electronic billing system in all their supermarket outlets. This facilitates transparency in billing on the one hand, and relatively quick processing of cash transaction on the other. When we asked supermarket customers whether they had to wait for the purpose of billing, 72 per cent of the supermarket customers said that they did not have to wait while billing was being done (see Table 7.15a). The Hearty Mart group needs to think about why 28 per cent of the supermarket customers had to wait during billing and how the problem can be mitigated. But, overall, it does not appear to be a big concern for the Hearty Mart group. The reason is that if we look at Table 7.15b, we find that, on the whole, more than 92 per cent of the supermarket customers are satisfied with the electronic billing system. As far as the saral shops are concerned, more than 92 per cent of the customers have been found to be happy with the electronic billing system (see Table 7.15a).

Table 7.15a

Do you have to Wait for Your Bill at Hearty Mart?

Do You Have to Wait for Your Bill?	*Supermarket*		*Saral Shop*		*Total*	
	No. of Customer	*Per cent*	*No. of Customer*	*Per cent*	*No. of Customer*	*Per cent*
Yes	84	28	74	92.5	158	41.58
No	216	72	6	7.5	222	58.42
Total	300	100	80	100	380	100.00

Table 7.15b

Are You Happy with Electronic Billing System of the Supermarket?

Are You Happy with Electronic Billing System?	*No. of Customer*	*Per cent*
Happy with electronic billing	278	92.67
Unhappy with electronic billing	22	7.33
Total	300	100.00

Display of the Items and their Cleanliness

The retail shops in rural areas are often not found as clean as their counterparts in urban areas. Hence, cleanliness in rural stores may be considered one of the key determinants of consumers' attention towards the store. Not only the storekeeper should keep their items clean but he should also keep the racks to be cleaned. In supermarket, the customers are allowed to enter into the store, to go directly to the rack, and to pick up the items they want to purchase. Hence, maintaining a store's overall cleanliness is important. Also, maintaining cleanliness helps creating a value in the minds of the individuals involved. Thus, through maintaining cleanliness, the Hearty Mart stores want to create such important value in the rural areas where they have already set up their retail outlets. This is somewhat reflected in the response of the customers, which is presented in Table 7.16. More than 93 per cent of the total number of customers of Hearty Mart supermarkets said that they found the goods and racks in the stores to be clean. As far as the saral shop customers are concerned, the proportion accounts for 100 per cent of the customers (not shown in the table). Such overwhelming response indicates that the customers are really impressed by the cleanliness factor which is often not experienced in other retail stores in rural areas.

Table 7.16

Do You Find the Goods in Racks Clean or Dusty?

Do You Find the Goods in Racks Clean or Dusty?	*No. of Customer*	*Per cent*
Clean	280	93.33
Dusty	20	6.67
Total	300	100.00

Availability of Credit

Credit is an important aspect of rural retail market. Almost all the rural informal retail stores allow the customers to purchase items on credit if that is sought for. But the formal stores such as supermarkets do not generally provide credit facility. In the cities, the customers are often found to subscribe to credit cards of different banking and financial organisations and thus meet their need of availing credit facilities. Due to relatively low purchasing power of the rural inhabitants, similar types of credit facilities are generally not seen to be availed by them. At this backdrop, it is interesting to note that most of the Hearty Mart supermarkets are experiencing growth while only a little more than 18 per cent of the total number of customers are found to have been allowed to purchase items on credit (see Table 7.17). This means that credit is not the only criterion that pulls customers to a store. It is quite a different experience as far as the saral shops are concerned. Table 7.17 suggests that 95 per cent of the customers of saral shops receive credit facility. As regards credit, it is evident that the Hearty Mart group has a dual policy—i.e. a strict policy for the supermarket customers and a liberal policy for saral shop customers. This is perhaps because of the fact that most of the saral shops are located in very remote villages. A strictly formal approach may result in low growth of the retail stores, because other retail stores often allow the low income people residing in the locality to purchase items on credit. From this perspective, the dual policy that has been adopted by the Hearty Mart group seems to appear realistic.

Table 7.17

Are the Items Available on Credit?

Are the Items Available on Credit?	*Supermarket*		*Saral Shop*		*Total*	
	No. of Customer	*Per cent*	*No. of Customer*	*Per cent*	*No. of Customer*	*Per cent*
Yes	55	18.33	76	95	131	34.47
No	232	77.33	3	3.75	235	61.84
No Opinion	13	4.33	1	1.25	14	3.68
Total	300	100	80	100	380	100.00

Customers' Responses about Hearty Mart Staff

As far as the supermarket concept is concerned, the behaviour of the staff (how they deal with the customers, how they answer to the queries of the customers, etc.) is one of the important determinants of growth of a supermarket store. In a small retail store, the shopkeeper or the owner is responsible to answer to the questions asked by the customers. In a supermarket, the staff members are the representatives of the store owner. It is their responsibility to satisfy all the queries made by the customers and cooperate with them for easy purchasing experience. According to Table 7.18, as many as 99 per cent of the customers of the Hearty Mart supermarkets are found to have been satisfied by the responses and cooperation extended by the staff members when they wanted to know something from them. In case of saral shops, the proportion accounts for more than 96 per cent (see Table 7.18). This indicates that the staff members of the Hearty Mart organisation have been groomed well and thus they are facilitating the growth of the organisation as desired by their leaders.

Table 7.18

Do You Get Cooperation and Satisfactory Response to Your Queries from the Hearty Mart Staff?

Do You Get Cooperation and Satisfactory Response to Your Queries from the Staff?	*Supermarket*		*Saral Shop*		*Total*	
	No. of Customer	*Per cent*	*No. of Customer*	*Per cent*	*No. of Customer*	*Per cent*
Yes	297	99	77	96.25	374	98.42
No	3	1	3	3.75	6	1.58
Total	300	100	80	100	380	100.00

Conclusion

In this chapter, we have analysed the data collected from the customers of the Hearty Mart stores. Some of the main findings of the analyses are summarised below. The shopping pattern illustrates that the large proportion of customers prefer to complete their shopping at Hearty Mart stores within five visits in a month. The households belonging to low-income strata account for a significant proportion of customers of the Hearty Mart stores. An interesting observation was found when we compared the perspective of the customers between Hearty Mart stores and other stores. While it is evident that a considerable proportion of the customers do visit other stores as well, a very significant proportion of the total number of respondents have been found to have reduced visiting other stores in the recent past since they have found Hearty Mart stores as their favourite shopping destinations. As far as some components of social entrepreneurship are concerned, what do we hear from the customers? For both Hearty Mart supermarkets and saral shops, high proportions of customers have found the discounts provided by the Hearty Mart stores on different items to be greater than that of other stores. Also, in the case of quality of products sold by Hearty Mart stores, most of the customers have found their products better than that sold by other stores. This indicates that Hearty Mart stores have so far been able to create a more-or-less good impression among the rural customers. In terms of quality, services, and other facilities, Hearty Mart is creating a new value (new shopping concept without compromising quality) in the retail markets in rural Gujarat. Generally, the urban customers are value conscious and retailers are found to meet the urban customers' demands for 'value'. As regards rural areas, the Hearty Mart organisation is taking steps so that such value is not ignored in the case of the rural retail customers.

Appendix A-7.1

Store Locations and Number of Samples

Type of Retail Outlet	*Store Location*	*No. of Customers Interviewed*
Supermarket	Vadgam	50
	Chhapi	50
	Juhapura	50
	Surat	50
	Dholka	50
	Meta	50
	Total	300
Saral Shops	Jethipura	20
	Pipodar	20
	Kanai	20
	Ilol	20
	Total	80

Note: Currently, there are 13 franchisees associated with Hearty Mart. However, we have conducted surveys in 10 franchisees as stated in this table.

8

Concluding Observations

Introduction

This study is concerned with a community-oriented business network which is functioning as a retail/supermarket franchising model in the state of Gujarat (mainly in rural areas). The network is functioning under the banner of 'Hearty Mart'—an organisation which is the brainchild of Nadeem Jafri, the franchiser-entrepreneur, who first founded a supermarket in Juhapura area in Ahmedabad in 2004. He belongs to the family of the Syed Jafri sect-head of the Shia Momin community. His religious superior position in his community has given him an opportunity to build a 'community-oriented' franchising network (i.e. a network that has engaged his community people as franchisees) of the Hearty Mart supermarket chain.

As said, the Hearty Mart Supermarket at Juhapura, which is the franchiser, has established franchising networks with several franchisees across the state. The franchisees are geographically dispersed in remote rural areas. Through their relationship, the franchisees are allowed to use the 'Hearty Mart' brand and, in exchange, the franchisees are liable to pay franchisee fees to the franchiser. In addition, the franchiser takes some responsibilities to promote business of its franchisees through the help of its FDC (franchisee development cell). The FDC provides all the franchisees with necessary guidance and support in order to develop the village level supermarkets or saral shops of proper standard as has been set by the franchiser. The guidance and support include providing ideas about product packaging, presentation of the store, management of inventory and accounts management. Additionally, being a part of the Hearty Mart system, the franchisee gets access to the services of

Hearty Mart Enterprise (HME). There is another body within Hearty Mart called CG (corporate group). The CG takes care of the issues as far as the wholesale marketing of various products of Hearty Mart's own brand (e.g. HME, Hearty Mart Celesta, Hearty Mart Tea-Packers, etc.) is concerned. The FDC takes care of the issues as far as the retail marketing strategies of the Hearty Mart franchisees are concerned.

In this respect, let us not forget to mention that the underlying foundation of the bonding between the franchiser and the franchisees has something to do with their religious connection. As indicated earlier, a common thing observed among all the franchisees is that they all belong to the Chilea community. Although being a Chilea is not a mandatory requirement to become a franchisee of the Hearty Mart, the Hearty Mart franchising, however, has been possible for the direct involvement of some entrepreneurs of this particular sect. The franchiser-entrepreneur, Nadeem Jafri, who himself belongs to the sect-head of this community facilitated this network development. One big advantage of building such religion or community-based network is that adequate trust which is an important component of any business relationship and is generally thought to be present between the agents.

Within the framework of the Hearty Mart franchising system, the Juhapura unit plays the central role and coordinates different functions in the network. The subordinate entities (i.e. Hearty Mart franchisees) retain their autonomy as far as daily operations are concerned, but have to follow directions and standards imposed on them by the superior entity (Hearty Mart Juhapura). From the formal viewpoint, the interdependence actually exists only between the franchiser and the franchisee. Individual franchisees are independent of one another, since no exchange of resources takes place among them. Of course, franchisee entities exchange information in the meetings organised by the coordinator. However, as already indicated, the network coordinator plays the most important role in formulating strategies, specifying the ways of utilising resources, establishing norms, and so on. Subordinate entities which enter the franchisee system are informed about all necessary details of its functioning.

Social Aspects

Social entrepreneurs think of business and profits, but at the same time, they want to improve the life of the deprived people too. People involved in this franchising business do not have any faith in charity or philanthropy. Now, if they continue to look after the interest of the poor, they will be able to blend the concept of social entrepreneurship with the model of supermarket franchising chains. The Islamic perspective concerning ethical aspects of business enterprise is also an interesting matter. The ethical aspects are made up of five axioms, namely, trust, justice, sincerity, truthfulness, and benevolence. At least some of these have some links with the components of social entrepreneurship. For example, as far as justice is concerned, an Islamic entrepreneur, just like a social entrepreneur, takes care of the poor customers by controlling his personal desire for extremely high return, i.e. by offering them products at very reasonable price.

In the light of some important pillars of social entrepreneurship (as stated chapter 3 and chapter 5), we have studied the role of Nadeem and the role of Hearty Mart in initiating some changes in some rural areas of Gujarat. Our findings suggest that Nadeem has played a pioneering role in facilitating the setting up of supermarket-style retail outlets in rural Gujarat and thereby allowing rural poor to experience modern shopping at their localities within their affordability. Hearty Mart has customer base of low and lower-middle income groups and thus its main objective has been to serve them with the best available quality at the lowest available prices. Also, Nadeem's initiative motivated some villagers of farming community to join his hands as franchisees and build a strong franchising network. This has created further opportunity of employment for the local, rural, unemployed youth in the rural retail supermarkets. More importantly, the franchiser and the franchisees are not seen to be doing any philanthropy; they are following efficiently the market principles and thus, their scalability is not being hindered. Through the help of various mechanisms (as described in chapter 5), the franchisees are selling products at discounted prices and this is helping them to excel in terms of scalability.

Organisational Aspects

Hearty Mart is operating and functioning in the market. Both the franchiser and the franchisee deal with several things for which they opt for market transaction. But since market is not the solution to all the economic problems, the franchising model which builds on a coordination mechanism within a new 'organisational framework' at the backdrop of rural-urban duality is the main focus of this study. Setting up of supermarkets—even in small-scale—in the rural areas by the rural Chilea entrepreneurs would have been extremely difficult if Nadeem, the franchiser, had not joined their hands. Thus, coordination (and cooperation) between franchiser and franchisee plays an important role in this model.

Information may be needed for additional purposes as well. For example, different types of information may be useful for the generation of innovative ideas. Sometimes ingenuity and resources would be required to achieve the social development of the community members involved.

Let us have a look at information creation in retail markets—for instance, Hearty Mart. How does an individual retail-franchisee draw attention of the people to the quality of the products in his shop? One may be curious about why the various products are displayed so differently. We submit that a major reason for these differences is the variation in quality that may be expected from different brands.

However, the interesting finding we get is that even an organisational strategy as an alternative is not going to yield desired results if some other basic problems (e.g. low level of education) are not properly addressed. We believed that a well developed organisation and its internal network would be found to be a way-out to the problem of underdevelopment. As far as most of the franchisees are concerned, the organisation itself appears to be a mechanism to tackle the price-centered information problem. However, the case of Surat franchisee explains that organisational mechanism cannot be proved to be properly functioning if some basic problems such as lack of self-confidence or lack of minimum education (i.e. the problem of bounded rationality) are not remedied.

Institutional Aspects

Hearty Mart Franchisee system represents a model which has grown based on religious-institutional links. As we know, religion often plays important institutional role. Especially, people who belong to the particular cultural and business section within the Islamic religion (e.g. Sufi and business minded Shias/Chileas) have strong fellow feeling and community bonding. The main factor associated with such bond is 'institutional trust'. Hence, the social capital that stems from the trust that is present among the members of the Chilea community is the building block of the formation and proliferation of Hearty Mart franchisee model. The institutional trust has played some role in both the spheres—i.e. in the relationship between the franchiser and the franchisee, and in the relationship between the franchisee and the customer.

Let us now look at another interesting point. How can one retailer gain trust of his customers? This can be done in several ways. For example, the retailer may offer good quality products, which can earn him some reputation as well as trust in the market. Also, personal rapport with the customers in the rural areas is an important factor. An organisational framework often helps in building the brand and thus reputation and trust as well. The Hearty Mart franchiser has been able to successfully pass on this message to their franchisees. The franchisees are also following the guidance. The nature of rural customer is very different from that of urban customers. The Hearty Mart franchisees are maintaining good rapport with their customers through personal interaction.

Concluding Remarks

The finding suggests that the households belonging to low-income strata account for a significant proportion of customers of the Hearty Mart stores. An interesting observation was found when we compared the perspective of the customers between Hearty Mart stores and other stores. While it is evident that a considerable proportion of the customers do visit other stores as well, a very significant proportion of the total number of respondents have been found to have reduced visiting other stores in the recent past since they have found Hearty Mart stores as their favourite shopping destinations. As far as some components of social entrepreneurship are concerned, what do we hear from the customers? For both Hearty Mart supermarkets and saral shops, high proportions of customers have found the discounts provided by the Hearty Mart stores on different items to be greater than that of other stores. Also, in the case of quality of products sold by Hearty Mart stores, most of the customers have found their products better than that sold by other stores. This indicates that Hearty Mart stores have so far been able to create a more-or-less good impression among the rural customers. In terms of quality, services, and other facilities, Hearty Mart is creating a new value (new shopping concept without compromising quality) in the retail markets in rural Gujarat. Generally, the urban customers are value conscious and retailers are found to meet the urban customers' demands for 'value'. As regards rural areas, the Hearty Mart organisation is taking steps so that such value is not ignored in the case of the rural retail customers.

References

Ab. Aziz, M.R. (2011) "Opportunity for Agro Entrepreneur in Developing Agro Initiative in Islamic Banking in Malaysia", *The Journal of Animal & Plant Sciences* 21(2): 290-302.

Abeng, T. (1997). "Business Ethics in Islamic Context: Perspectives of a Muslim Business Leader", *Business Ethics Quarterly* 7(3): 47-54.

Ahmad, S.F. (1991). "The Ethical Responsibility of Business: Islamic Principles and Implication", *Journal of Objective Studies* 3(1): 23-43.

Alagh, Munish (2014). "Organisational Aspects of a Franchising Model in Western India", An unpublished note. SPIESR.

Alagh, Munish and P.C. Bandhopadhya (2015). "A Case Study on Organised Retailing and Supply Chain Management System", A Paper presented at the *National Conference of Agricultural Marketing* at Anand, January.

Alagh, Munish and Jatin Christie (2009a). "Role of Proxemics in Entrepreneurship: A Case Study of Hearty Mart Supermarket", Paper presented at the *8th Biennial Conference*. Entrepreneurial Development Institute of India. March.

———. (2009b). "Social Entrepreneurship: Profits or/and Community", *12th Nirma International Conference on Management (NICOM)*, January. [Also published as: Alagh, Munish and Jatin Christie (2009). "Social Entrepreneurship—Profits or/and Community", in C. Gopalakrishnan, Nina Muncherji and Upinder Dhar (eds.), *Creating Wealth through Strategic HR and Entrepreneurship*. New Delhi: Excel Books].

———. (2011a). "Organisational Determinants of Retail Franchising into Rural Areas: A Case Study of Chilea Community", Paper presented in the *Ninth Biennial Conference on Entrepreneurship*. Entrepreneurship Development Institute of India. 16-18 February.

———. (2011b). "Development of Social Spaces through Infrastructural Development: Commodity Vision", *Journal of Takshashila Academy of Economic Research*, January.

Alagh, Munish, S.P. Thenmouzi and Abraham Babu (2008). "A Case Study on Hearty Mart Supermarket: Business Venturing Sustenance and Growth", Collection of Cases by Participants of 29th *Faculty Development Program*. Indian Institute of Management Ahmedabad. February.

Alchian, A.A. and R.A. Kessel (1962). "Competition, Monopoly, and the Pursuit of Pecuniary Gain", in H.G. Lewis (ed.), *Aspects of Labor Economics*. Princeton: Princeton University Press. pp.157-83.

Alchian, Armen A. (1965). "Some Economics of Property Rights", *Il Politico*: 816-29.

Alchian, Armen A. and Harold Demsetz (1972). "Production, Information Costs, and Economic Organization", *The American Economic Review* 62(5): 777-95.

al-Ghazali, A.H. (2006). *Collection of Letters*. Beirut: Dar Al-Fakr.

Allen, Douglas W. (2000). "Transaction Costs". In Boudewijn Bouckaert and Gerrit De Geest (eds.), *The Encyclopedia of Law and Economics,* (Volume 1). Chelthenham: Edward Elgar. pp.893-926.

Al-Misri, Rafiq Yunus (2007). *Al-Iqtisad wa al-Akhlaq*. Damascus: Dar al-Qalam.

Alonso, Ricardo, Wouter Dessein and Niko Matouschek (2008). "When Does Coordination Require Centralization?" *American Economic Review* 98(1): 145-79.

Al-Qaradawi, Yusuf (2001). *Dawr al-Qiyam wa-al-Akhlaq fi al-Iqtisad al-Islami.* Cairo: Maktabah Wahbah.

Alter, Sutia K. (2006). "Social Enterprise Models and their Mission and Money Relationships", *Social Entrepreneurship: New Models of Sustainable Social Change*: 205-32.

Alvord, Sarah H., L. David Brown and W. Christine Letts (2004). "Social Entrepreneurship and Societal Transformation", *The Journal of Applied Behavioral Science* 40(3): 260-82.

Alvord, S.H., L.D. Brown and C.W. Letts (2004). "Social Entrepreneurship and Social Transformation: An Exploratory Study", *Working Paper* No. 15. The Hauser Center for Nonprofit Organizations, Harvard University.

Anderlini, Luca and Leonardo Felli (2004). "Bounded Rationality and Incomplete Contracts", *Research in Economics* 58(1): 3-30.

Arrow, K.E. (1974). *The Limits of Organization*. W.W. Norton & Company.

Arrow, K.J. (1970). "Political and Economic Evaluation of Social Effects and Externalities", in J. Margolis (ed.), *The Analysis of Public Output*. New York: Columbia University Press. pp.1-23

————. (1985). "Informational Structure of the Firm", *American Economic Review* 75(2): 303-07.

Audretsch, D.B. (1995). *Innovation and Industry Evolution.* Cambridge: MIT Press.

Austin, J.E. and E. Reficco (2009). "Corporate Social Entrepreneurship", *Working Paper.* Harvard: Harvard Business School.

Austin, J., H. Stevenson, and J. Wei-Skillern (2006). "Social and Commercial Entrepreneurship: Same, Different, or Both?" *Entrepreneurship Theory and Practice* 31(1): 1–22.

Awasthi, Dinesh (2010). "Promoting Social Entrepreneurship for Poverty Alleviation: The Indian Experience", *Keynote Paper* in plenary session 3 'Integrating TVET Skills Development with Social Entrepreneurship' in the International Symposium on TVET Skills for Poverty Alleviation (TVET-SPAQ 2010), organised by the Colombo Plan Staff College for Technician Education (CPSC) held at Manila on 2-3 August.

Bardhan, Pranab K. (1980). "Interlocking Factor Markets and Agrarian Development: A Review of Issues", *Oxford Economic Papers* 32(1): 82-98.

Beekun, R.I. (1997). *Islamic Business Ethics.* Virginia: The International Institute of Islamic Thought.

Bell, David E. and Howard Raiffa (1988). *Decision-making: Descriptive, Normative, and Prescriptive Interactions.* Cambridge University Press.

Besley, Timothy (1995). "Property Rights and Investment Incentives: Theory and Evidence from Ghana", *Journal of Political Economy* 103(5): 903-37.

Borhan, J.T. Bin and M.R. Ab. Aziz (2009). "Agriculture and Agribusiness from the Perspective of Al-qur'an and Al-sunnah", *Jurnal Usuluddin* 30: 325-44.

Bruni, L., L. Corazzini and L. Stanca (2009). "Testing Theories of Reciprocity: Do Motivation Matter?" Journal of Economic Behaviour & Organization 71(2): 233-45.

Burlow, J., J. Geanakoplos and P. Klemperer (1985). "Multimarket Oligopoly: Strategic Substitutes and Complements", Journal of Political Economy 93(3): 488-511.

Chandra, Pankaj and Devanath Tirupati (2003). *Business Strategies for Managing Complex Supply Chains in Large Emerging Economies: The Story of AMUL.* A Report Prepared on Behalf of the

Indian Institute of Management, Ahmedabad.

Child, J. and D. Faulkner (1998). *Strategies of Co-operation: Managing Alliances, Networks, and Joint Ventures*. Oxford: Oxford University Press.

Coase, Ronald (1988). *The Firm, The Market and The Law*. Chicago: The University of Chicago.

———. (1960). "The Problem of Social Cost", *Journal of Law and Economics* 3(1): 1-44.

Cole, A.H. (1949). "Entrepreneurship and Entrepreneurial History", in A.H. Cole (ed.), *Change and the Entrepreneur: Postulates and Patterns for Entrepreneurial History*. Cambridge, M.A.: Harvard University Press. pp.85-96.

Cullen, J.B. and K.P. Parboteeah (2008). *Multinational Management: A Strategic Approach*. Mason, OH: South-Western Publishing.

Dasgupta, P. (1988). "Trust as a Commodity", in D. Gambetta (ed.), *Trust: Making and Breaking Cooperative Relations*. Oxford: Blackwell. pp.49-72.

Dees, G. (1998). "The Meaning of Social Entrepreneurship", *http://www.fuqua.duke.edu/centers/case/documents/dees_SE.pdf*. Last accessed on 30 October 2004.

Diaz-Bernardo, R. (2012). "An Analysis of Three Confronting Theories to Explain Franchising Supply", *Journal of Business & Economics Research* 10(3): 167-70.

Douma, Sytse and Hein Schreuder (2008). *Economic Approaches to Organizations*. 4th ed. London: Financial Times/Prentice Hall.

Drayton, Bill (2002). The Citizen Sector: Becoming as Entrepreneurial and Competitive as Business, *California Management Review* 44(3): 120-32.

Eggertsson, Thrainn (1990). *Economic Behaviour and Institutions*. Cambridge: Cambridge University Press.

Emerson, J. and P. Economy (2001). *Enterprising Non-Profits: A Toolkit for Social Entrepreneurs*. New York: Wiley Non-Profit Series.

Falk, Armin, Simon Gachter and Kovacs Judit (1999). "Intrinsic Motivation and Optimal Intensive Contracts", *Journal of Economic Psychology* 20(3): 251-284.

Fowler, A. (2000). "NGDOs as a Moment in History: Beyond Aid to Social Entrepreneurship or Civic Innovation?", Third World Quarterly 21(4): 637-54.

Geertz, C. (1978). "The Bazaar Economy: Information and Search in Peasant Marketing", *American Economic Review* 68(2): 28-32.

Germak, Andrew J. and Karun K. Singh (2009). "Social Entrepreneurship: Changing the Way Social Workers Do Business", *Administration in Social Work* 34(1): 79-95.

Hamid, Abdul and Zarrina Sa'ari (2011). "Reconstructing Entrepreneur's Development Based on al-Qur'an and al-Hadith", *International Journal of Business and Social Science* 2(19): 110-16.

Haniffa, R. (2002). "Social Responsibility Disclosure: An Islamic Perspective", *Indonesian Management and Accounting Journal* 1(2): 128-46.

Hannafey, F.T. (2003). "Entrepreneurship and Ethics: A Literature Review", *Journal of Business Ethics* 46(2): 99-110.

Hart, Oliver and Bengt Holmstrom (1986). "The Theory of Contracts", *Working Paper* 418. USA: Department of Economics, Massachusetts Institute of Technology (MIT).

Hasanuzzaman, S.M. (2003). *Islam and Business Ethics*. London: Institute of Islamic Banking and Insurance.

Hayami, Yujiro and Keijiro Otsuka (1993). *The Economics of Contract Choice: An Agrarian Perspective*. Clarendon Press.

Hayami, Yujiro (1997). *Development Economics, From the Poverty to the Wealth of Nations*. Oxford: Clarendon Press.

Hill, C. (2008). *Global Business Today*. New York: Irwin McGraw-Hill.

James, L.K. (2010). "Social Entrepreneurship as a Bottom-Up Model of Socio-Economic Development", *Development Outreach*. World Bank Institute. pp.16-18.

Jensen, M. (1983). "Organisation Theory and Methodology", *Accounting Review* 50(2): 319-39.

Klein, B. (1995). "The Economics of Franchise Contracts", *Journal of Corporate Finance* 2(1): 9-37.

Klein, Benjamin, Robert Crawford and Armen Alchian (1978). "Vertical Integration, Appropriable Rents, and the Competitive Contracting Process", *Journal of Law and Economics* 21(2): 297-326.

Klewes, Joachim and Robert Wreschniok (eds.) (2010). *Reputation Capital: Building and Maintaining Trust in the 21st Century*; USA: Springer.

Ludwig, T.M. (2001). *The Sacred Paths: Upper Saddle River*. NJ: Prentice Hall.

Mair, Johanna and Ignasi Martí (2006). "Social Entrepreneurship Research: A Source of Explanation, Prediction, and Delight", *Journal of World Business* 41(1): 36-44.

Manan, S.K.A. and M.A. Abdullah (2012). "Perception of Small-and Medium-sized Enterprises in Klang Valley, Malaysia Towards Profit and Loss Sharing Mode of Financing", *Malaysian Journal of Economic Studies* 49(1): 37-48.

Matthews, R.C.O. (1986). "The Economics of Institutions and the Sources of Growth", *Economic Journal* 96(4): 903-10.

McClaren, N. (2013). "The Personal Selling and Sales Management Ethics Research: Managerial Implications and Research Directions from a Comprehensive Review of the Empirical Literature", *Journal of Business Ethics* 112(1): 101-25.

McKnight, D.H. and N.L. Chervany (1996). "The Meaning of Trust" (Published online) (Retrieved 23 September 2012), *http://misrc.umn.edu/wpaper/WorkongPapers/9604*.

Mehmet, M.A. (1997). "Al-Ghazzali on Social Justice", *International Journal of Social Economics* 24(11): 1203-18.

Milgrom, Paul and John Roberts (1992). *The Economics, Organisation and Management*. NJ: Prentice Hall.

Mitronen, Lasse and Kristian Möller (2001). *Management of Hybrid Organizations: A Case Study of a Retailing 'Network Organization'*. A Competitive Paper for IMP. Finland: Helsinki School of Economics and Business Administration.

Mort, G.S., J. Weerawardena and K. Carnegie (2002). "Social Entrepreneurship: Towards Conceptualization and Measurement", *American Marketing Association Conference Proceedings* 13(5).

Muhammad, M.Z., A. Ilias, M.F. Ghazali, R.C. Abdullah and H. Amin (2008). "An Analysis of Islamic Ethics in Small and Medium Enterprise", *UNITAR, an E-journal* 4: 46-58.

Murphy, Patrick J. and Susan M. Coobes (2009). "A Model of Social Entrepreneurial Discovery", *Journal of Business Ethics* 87(3): 325-336.

Nagler, J. (2007). *Is Social Entrepreneurship Important for Economic Development Policies*? Sydney: University of New South Wales.

Narayanan, Dinesh (2012). "Backstreet Superstore", *Forbes India*, February.

Nicholls, A. (2008). "Introduction", in A. Nicholls (ed.), *Social Entrepreneurship: New Models of Sustainable Social Change*. Oxford, England: Oxford University Press. pp.1–35.

Nicholls, A. and A.H. Cho (2008). "Social Entrepreneurship: The Structuration of a Field", in A. Nicholls (ed.), *Social Entrepreneurship: New Models of Sustainable Social Change*. Oxford, England: Oxford University Press. pp.99–118.

North, D.C. (1990). *Institutions, Institutional Change and Economic Performance*. Cambridge, Cambridge University Press.

Nystén-Haarala, Soili, Nari Lee, and Jukka Lehto (2010). "Flexibility in Contract Terms and Contracting Processes", *International Journal of Managing Projects in Business* 3(3): 462-78.

OECD (2011). *Science, Technology and Industry Scoreboard: Innovation and Growth in Knowledge Economies*; Paris: OECD.

Omrane, Amina (2013). "Social Entrepreneurship and Sustainable Development: The Role of Business Models", *Working Paper.* EMLYON Business School. March . Electronic copy available at: *http://ssrn.com/abstract=2232438.*

Oukil, M-Said (2013). "Entrepreneurship and Entrepreneurs in an Islamic Context", *Journal of Islamic and Human Advanced Research* 3(3): 115-30.

Pauly, Mark V. (1968). "The Economics of Moral Hazard: Comment", *American Economic Review* 58(3): 531-37.

Peredo, Ana Maria and Murdith McLean (2006). "Social Entrepreneurship: A Critical Review of the Concept", *Journal of World Business* 41(1): 56-65.

Popoviciu, Ioan and Salomea A. Popoviciu (2011). "Social Entrepreneurship, Social Enterprise and the Principles of a Community of Practice", *Revista de Cercetare si Interventie Socială* 33: 44-55.

Porter, Michael E. (1988). *Creating and Sustaining Superior Performance.* New York: Free Press.

Putnam, Robert D. (1993). "The Prosperous Community: Social Capital and Public Life", *The American Prospect* 13: 35-42 (Spring). Also available at: *http://epn.org/prospect/13/13putn.html*

Rennick, S.A. (2013). "Personal Grievance Sharing, Frame Alignment, and Hybrid Organizational Structures: The Role of Social Media in North Africa's 2011 Uprisings", *Journal of Contemporary African Studies* 31(2): 156-4.

Robbins, Lionel (1935). *An Essay on the Nature of the Significance of Economic Science.* 2nd Edition. London: Macmillan & Co.

Roberts, D. and C. Woods (2005). "Changing the World on a Shoestring: The Concept of Social Entrepreneurship", *University of Auckland Business Review:* 45-51, (Autumn.

Roper, J. and G. Cheney (2005). "The Meanings of Social Entrepreneurship Today", *Corporate Governance* 5(3): 95-104.

Ross, S.A. (1973). "The Economic Theory of Agency: The Principal's Problem", *American Economic Review* 63(2): 134-39.

Roy, Abhijit, Alan Brumagim and Irene Goll (2013). "Predictors of Social Entrepreneurship Success: A Cross-national Analysis of Antecedent Factors", *Journal of Social Entrepreneurship* 5(1): 42-59.

Rubin, Paul H. (1978). "The Theory of the Firm and the Structure of the Franchise Contract", *The Journal of Law & Economics* 21(1): 223-33.

Salamzadeh, Aidin, Yashar Salamzadeh and Mehran Nejati (2011). "Social Entrepreneurship: Analyzing Literature and Proposing a Comprehensive Model", Paper presented at The 9th Asian Academy of Management International Conference, 14-16 October. Accessed from: *http://www.academia.edu/1019416/Social_Entrepreneurship_Analyzing_Literature_and_Proposing_ a_Comprehensive_Model*

Schumpeter, Joseph A. (1934). *Theory of Economic Development: An Inquiry into Profits, Capital, Credit, Interest and the Business Cycle*. Cambridge: Harvard University Press.

Scott, Shane (1996). "Hybrid Organisational Arrangements and Their Implications for Finn Growth and Survival: A Study of New Franchisors", *Academy of Management Journal* 39(1): 216-34.

Seabright, P. (1993). "Managing Local Commons: Theoretical Issues in Incentive Design", *Journal of Economic Perspectives* 7(4): 113-34.

———. (2004). *The Company of Strangers: A Natural History of Economic Life*. Princeton: Princeton University Press.

Seelos, Christian and Johanna Mair (2005). "Social Entrepreneurship: Creating New Business Models to Serve the Poor", *Business Horizons* 48(3): 241-46.

Shaharuddin, A. (2005). "Islamic Business Ethics: A Managerial Perspective", Proceedings of the *Malaysian Finance Association 7th Annual Conference*. 9-10 May. Kuala Terengganu.

Swanson, L.A. and D.D. Zhang (2010). "The Social Entrepreneurship Zone", *Journal of Nonprofit & Public Sector Marketing* 22(2): 71-88.

Talukdar, Tapash (2009). "Bridging a Retail Divide", *The Economic Times*, Mumbai. October.

Thaker, Mitul (2008). "Unexplored Areas Catch Retail Attention", *Economic Times*, Ahmedabad. 29 March.

Trivedi, Hemant and Nadeem Jafri (2008). *Creating a Retail Brand*. This case study on 'Hearty Mart Retail Supermarket' was published by The Case Centre (formerly known as the European Case Clearing House), UK registered office is at Cranfield University, and USA registered office is at Babson College.

Trivedi, C. (2010). "Towards a Social Ecological Framework for Social Entrepreneurship", *Journal of Entrepreneurship* 19(1): 63-80.

Trivedi, Divya (2009). "Mart with a Rural Heart", *Hindu Business Line*, April.

Turek, I. (2007). "Charactristics of Franchise Enterprises as Network Organization", *Annales Universitatis Apulensis: Series Oeconomica* 2(9): 426-30.

Wallace, S.L. (1999). "Social Entrepreneurship: The Role of Social Purpose Enterprises in Facilitating Community Economic Development", *Journal of Developmental Entrepreneurship* 4(2): 153-74.

Williamson, O.E. (2010). "Transaction Cost Economics: The Natural Progression", *Journal of Retailing* 86(3): 215-26.

World Commission on Environment and Development (1987). *Our Common Future*. Oxford, UK: Oxford University Press.

Yaacob, Yazilmiwati and Ilhaamie Abdul Ghani Azmi (2012). "Entrepreneurs' Personality from Islamic Perspective: A Study of Successful Muslim Entrepreneurs in Malaysia", *International Proceedings of Economics Development and Research* 46(16): 86-90.

Zahir, Jan Mohamed (2013). "The Adrenalin of Adversity", *Open Magazine*, April 29.

Zahra, Shaker A., Eric Gedajlovic, Donald O. Neubaum and Joel M. Shulman (2009). "A Typology of Social Entrepreneurs: Motives, Search Processes and Ethical Challenges", *Journal of Business Venturing* 24(5): 519–532.